Will Campbell, Preacher Man

Essays in the Spirit of a Divine Provocateur

Will Campbell, Preacher Man

Essays in the Spirit of a Divine Provocateur

Kyle Childress &
Rodney Wallace Kennedy

FOREWORD BY
Stanley Hauerwas

CASCADE *Books* · Eugene, Oregon

WILL CAMPBELL, PREACHER MAN

Essays in the Spirit of a Divine Provocateur

Copyright © 2016 Wipf and Stock Publishers. All rights reserved. Except for brief quotations in critical publications or reviews, no part of this book may be reproduced in any manner without prior written permission from the publisher. Write: Permissions, Wipf and Stock Publishers, 199 W. 8th Ave., Suite 3, Eugene, OR 97401.

Cascade Books
An Imprint of Wipf and Stock Publishers
199 W. 8th Ave., Suite 3
Eugene, OR 97401
www.wipfandstock.com

Paperback ISBN 978-1-4982-0273-2
Hardback ISBN 978-1-4982-0275-6
Ebook ISBN 978-1-4982-0274-9

Cataloging-in-Publication data:

Names: Childress, Kyle, and Rodney Wallace Kennedy.

Title: Will Campbell, preacher man : essays in the spirit of a divine provocateur / Kyle Childress and Rodney Wallace Kennedy.

Description: Eugene, OR : Cascade Books, 2016 | Includes bibliographical references.

Identifiers: ISBN 978-1-4982-0273-2 (paperback) | 978-1-4982-0275-6 (hardback) | 978-1-4982-0274-9 (ebook)

Subjects: 1. Campbell, Will D., 1924–2013. 2. Church work. III. Reconciliation. I. Title.

Classification: HV7407 .C535 2016 (print)

Manufactured in the U.S.A.

Contents

Foreword by Stanley Hauerwas | vii

Introduction | xi

PART I : ESSAYS BY KYLE CHILDRESS AND RODNEY WALLACE KENNEDY

Will Campbell: In Memoriam | 3

Texan and Comanche | 5

Two Christianities | 8

Old Pickups and Advent | 11

Porching, Friendship and Ministry | 14

Truth Dazzles Gradually | 17

Out of the Old Rock | 20

Will Campbell, Reconciliation, and Us | 23

The Hood Abides | 26

I'm a Preacher | 29

Preaching Is a Sacrament | 33

A Truth Serum? | 39

God Is Not Scary | 41

Everybody's a Critic | 43

What's a Southern Boy Doing in Dayton, Ohio? | 45

I Am a Redneck | 47

Why It Is Christian to Oppose Government-Sponsored Worship in Public Schools | 49

McKnight's Dry Goods Store | 53

There's No Business Like Church Business | 55

Made a Preacher at Twelve | 57

The Parsonage: Where You Can't Make this Stuff Up! | 60

Evolution as Faith Partner | 65

CONTENTS

A Meal | 68
Choose Your Dayton | 73
Goodness Trumps Rights | 76
Lies about the Bible and Gays | 79
A Baptism | 81
The Doxology of Creation | 83
We Have a Jordan to Cross Again and Again | 86

PART II: SELECTED SERMONS

Sermons by Kyle Childress
The Power of Weakness and the Weakness of Power | 91
Who's Arresting Whom? | 98
We Can Breathe | 104

Sermons by Rodney Wallace Kennedy
Is America Humanly and Civilly Bankrupt? | 110
What Have We Done with the Good News? | 115
The Gospel Is Relevant | 122
Bibliography | 129

Foreword

Stanley Hauerwas

This book of short, profound, punchy, funny essays by Kyle Childress and Rodney Wallace Kennedy is in honor of Will Campbell. Childress and Kennedy know they are not, nor do they pretend to be, Will Campbell. Indeed they know well any presumption that it might be possible to be Will Campbell means you did not know Will Campbell well. Moreover, if there was anything Will Campbell hated it was pretense. Will Campbell never pretended to be, say, or do anything. What you saw in Will Campbell was what you got. Will Campbell might have had some fun with you but he would never be or say something that suggested he might be different than what he said or did.

So you might wonder why Childress and Kennedy think this book might honor Campbell. There are few essays on Campbell in the book but every essay in the book reflects what Childress and Kennedy have learned from Campbell. Accordingly, Childress and Kennedy give us Campbell-like reflections about the everyday life of ministers and the people they serve and lead. These are lovely concrete depictions of their lives as Baptist pastors and the people whom they encounter because they are Baptist pastors. Childress, for example, introduces us to Dude Templeton, an estimable lady who Sunday after Sunday is always there, that is, in church. I cannot help but think that Dude is the kind of person Campbell would have loved to know.

Though they have not tried to be Will Campbell, what Childress and Kennedy have given us clearly reflects Campbell's influence. That influence can be characterized in a number of ways but I think at the heart of this book, at the heart of Will Campbell, is the virtue of patience. Driving a pickup on its last legs takes patience. To be in the ministry confronted by people who just do not get it takes time. To learn to play the piano requires perseverance. To have the wisdom honed, as Campbell's was, from the everyday is hard won. Indeed a wisdom born of patience was at the heart of Will Campbell's work and it is equally the heart of these essays.

So I think Childress and Kennedy are right to think Campbell would have been honored by this book. He probably would not have made much of the word "honored," but he would have enjoyed reading these honest reflections. At least one of the reasons, moreover, he would like the book is that it is not a book about him. Rather it is a book that deals and evokes a common world shared by Childress, Kennedy, and Campbell. That common world can be given a name. It is called "the South." It is a world that can even be found in a place called Texas although the forms the "South" takes there can be quite distinctive.

If he was anything Will Campbell was "the South." He was, of course, an original, which means that to say he was Southern does not do justice to the complex character of his life. But that is but a way to indicate he was a Southern original. He was not only a Southern original, he was a Baptist original. That he was such an original meant he went his own way during the integration struggle in the South. He was on the side of integration against those forces that would have preserved segregation. He was a man of courage who never felt the necessity to call attention to his being so because he was simply doing what he knew Jesus expected him to do.

I shall never forget the first time I saw him. It was at Yale Divinity School. Campbell had graduated from Yale Divinity School only to return to Mississippi to serve as the chaplain at the University of Mississippi during the struggle to integrate that school. He had been brought back to the Divinity School to give a lecture, a form of life he had little use for, about his work in Mississippi. The lecture was in the most formal room in the Divinity School, known as the "Common Room." The paintings of past Divinity School Deans hung on the walls of the Common Room. So Campbell began his lecture in great and good company.

He began by explaining he was chewing tobacco and he needed something in which to spit. He was given a Coke bottle, which he used with great facility. As a Texan at Yale I was impressed by his refusal to let the sophisticated folk in the Common Room determine who he should be. Perhaps even more important for me was his refusal to let us demonize the enemies of integration. He would not let us forget that Jesus had also died for opponents of integration.

What I saw in Campbell, what I think distinguishes the essays in this book to honor him, was the strong connection between the work of reconciliation and humor. Will Campbell was a very serious man who took great risks to integrate the schools of the South, but he did so with a spirit of humility born from a life that never failed to remind Christian and non-Christian alike that when all is said and done this is about Jesus. Childress and Kennedy do not let us forget Jesus. That they remember Jesus is why I think Campbell would have so liked this book. I cannot imagine higher praise for what Childress and Kennedy have given us in these witty and often quite challenging reflections.

Introduction

Will D. Campbell, preacher, pastor, storyteller, civil rights activist, provocateur, unofficial chaplain of country music, and thorn in the flesh of institutional Christianity, is a paradoxical figure in Southern religious and literary life. Will always insisted he didn't want any disciples and was known to chase more than one earnest seminarian away from his farm outside Nashville, Tennessee. We are disciples of Will D. Campbell. Now, we attempt to take up the mantle of Will and carry it as far down the road as possible. Whether Will would have approved or not is up in the air. He never "cottoned" to the idea of disciples.

Will's symbol was the floppy preacher's hat of an earlier era and he always said that he was just a preacher. Just a preacher? There's no such thing as just a preacher. We too are preachers.

Marshall Frady describes Will as one of God's "divine fools." We believe that Will was a twentieth-century version of St. Paul's "fool for Christ." The irony of "folly" comes across in Will's character, preaching, and writing. He dares to speak truth to power while celebrating the generosity of spirit, compassion, forgiveness, and courage of simple Christian faith.

As Will's friend, Walker Percy, put it *The Second Coming*, "Could it be that the Lord is here, masquerading behind this simple silly holy face?"

To use a different metaphor, from St. Paul's writings, Will was a "thorn in the flesh" of the institutional church, especially the Southern Baptist Convention. William Sloane Coffin, in a sermon, says, "A thorn is something we are stuck with." Some of us are called to be thorns in the flesh of the majority. No one chooses such a calling but it is carved out of our experiences and our education. We wake up one morning and know that we have been called to get up on the horse of dissent and ride like the wind. Or as the Rev. Alonzo Hickman in Ralph Ellison's *Juneteenth*, says to his protégé Hickman: "And the Master said, 'Hickman, Rise up on the Word and ride . . . . And Bliss, I threw back my head and rode! It was like a riddle or a joke, but if so, it was the Lord's joke and I was playing it straight. And maybe that's what a preacher really is, he's the Lord's own straight man."' The message: To all sinners, pure compassion; to all self-righteous, the wrath of critique. We offer this collection of essays and sermons as a memorial to Will Campbell. Will dealt with an array of favorite subjects: racial division, prisons, capital punishment, Congress, the Constitution and flag burning, secular politics, biblical certainty, capital punishment, women clergy, homeless/houseless persons, the First Amendment, submissive wives and Southern Baptist preachers, illegal aliens, the "R" word—redneck, war, boycotting Disney over gays, money, being a true conservative, human rights, prayer in public schools, topless bars, Bill Clinton's mess, marriage and happiness, Jews and Christians.

These essays are, simply put, two writers "unplugged" from the usual rigor of more academic writing. They are in the words of Will Campbell, whose style we have attempted to imitate, "a medley of little ditties." They are of various lengths and subject matters—humorous, ironic, combative, inspirational, and perhaps even a bit profound. They reflect at times whatever one of us was mad about in the morning when first reading the accounts of the comments and claims of various kinds of Baptists. As preachers made the news with outlandish claims or crazy actions, the temptation to pray, "O Lord, please let this one be a Methodist or a Presbyterian," was overwhelming.

Will insisted that he didn't want any disciples. We, taking the route of a Nicodemus or Joseph of Arimathea, have been secret disciples all these years. And now that Will has entered the new realm of eternity, we are publicly declaring that we are his disciples because he was so clearly a disciple of Jesus. Will, having imitated Jesus, and paying a huge price for doing so, is a saint that now deserves our imitation. Will, we love you! After all, what's not to love about a preacher who dared to call a certain species of Baptist preachers "those fat-cat false prophets"?

Our prayer is that the essays in Part I exemplify the spirit of Will D. Campbell, saint of almighty God. He is the kind of saint we would want to go to battle beside. After all, saints are often the toughest sort of people in the world. The sermons in Part II are offered as a tribute the Will as a preacher. While Will saw little remaining use for the "high steeple churches" the two of us are pastors of Baptist churches—in Dayton, Ohio and Nacogdoches, Texas. What we do, week after week, is write and deliver sermons. We offer these sermons not as models but as samples of how we struggle to be faithful to the Word and the words that we write. Most of all, it is our hope that this volume will encourage others to have the courage to speak truth to the powers and to dismantle the sacred cows. After all, from the golden calf of Exodus to the goose that lays the golden eggs in America, we have not made much progress. And someone ought always be there to raise the voice of the good news of Jesus Christ, the Son of God, in the face of all our golden idols. For us it is our calling, our true vocation and we revel in the ecstasy of the sermon.

PART I : Essays by Kyle Childress and
Rodney Wallace Kennedy

Will Campbell: In Memoriam

Kyle Childress

I had never heard of Will Campbell until the day I walked into a bookstore and saw a brand new novel called *The Glad River*, written by a Baptist preacher whom the dust jacket described as a "steeple dropout" and veteran civil rights activist.

I was a student pastor of a small rural Texas Baptist church. While I didn't know it yet, it was a good church. But at the time the church and I were in turmoil over the issue of race. At one point I had a shotgun pulled on me with the threat to blow my "nigger-loving head off"; in the year ahead I would have a man come after me in a congregational meeting to "whip the pastor's ass because I'm tired of his preaching on race."

After reading the dust jacket I didn't hesitate; I bought the book. I read *The Glad River* in three days and then cried for another three. I found a copy of Campbell's *Brother to a Dragonfly* and cried some more. Then I sat down and wrote a long letter to him about my struggle with my congregation over race, my struggle about remaining Baptist and my struggle with what seemed like almost everything.

In those days I was just discovering the works of Wendell Berry, John Howard Yoder, Stanley Hauerwas, Walter Brueggemann, and James Mc-Clendon and soaking in their ideas. Now Campbell came along, speaking to my heart in a way that unleashed the grief and joy of all the heady changes that were happening. When Campbell wrote back, I expected this prophet to call me to fight "the Enemy." Instead he encouraged me to love my enemies and discover that they are my neighbors, my sisters and brothers whom Christ has reconciled.

This "steeple dropout" didn't tell me to stay in this small steeple, but he came close. Whether I decided to go or to stay, he said, "The issue is not

3

right or wrong, justice or injustice, good or bad. It's human tragedy, and in a tragedy you can't take up sides. You just have to minister to the hurt wherever you find it." He continued: "Maybe some of your church members are assholes, but God loves them, and us, anyway," echoing the words that became among his most quoted.

"Well shit!" I thought. This was harder than I realized. I sat in a pew of that country church one night and cried some more.

Of course I made the pilgrimage up to his cabin in Mt. Juliet, outside of Nashville. I spent the day with him and William Stringfellow, who was also visiting and who further subverted my hopes of becoming a successful large-steeple pastor.

The result? For the last twenty-four years I've been the shepherd of a small steeple. After reading and believing what I learned from the likes of Will Campbell, Wendell Berry, and the rest, what choice did I have? About the time I came to Nacogdoches, I also linked up with five other Texas clergy to form "the Neighborhood," a group named after Will's small band of radical believers in *The Glad River*. Like the friends in the book, our friendship has renewed us, kept us sane, and even saved some lives.

I learned a lot about being a pastor from Will. I learned to hold the institutional church lightly, even a small one, and not take myself too seriously. As he liked to say, "God is God, and we're not."

I learned that no ministry, no service, no action is the gospel of Jesus Christ if it is not incarnated in flesh and blood community, relationship and friendship. For me, that means keeping it small, living in hope in the midst of tragedy, and ministering to the hurt wherever we find it.

At the conclusion of *The Glad River* two members of that Neighborhood bury the third member, and one gives this eulogy: "We had good times together. And bad. We laughed together and we cried together ... We confessed our cares in unlikely places. We worked and piddled, sat on rushing riverbanks in the hills, and whiled away many a summer afternoon on sleeping bayous. We read books and learned to talk like each other, argued about trivial things and took hard counsel together about the things that mattered ... But mostly ... we just loved one another."[1]

Will was this friend for me. He died just a month before his eighty-eighth birthday. I'll cry one more time.

---

1. Campbell, *Glad River*, 373.

Texan and Comanche

Kyle Childress

One of my earliest memories, faint and vague, is of being held by one of my parents at the dedication ceremony of a monument out on the north edge of my small West Texas hometown. It was 1959 and I was three years old, but we were there, along with most everyone else in town, for the unveiling of the Mackenzie Trail Historical Marker commemorating the 1874 route of Colonel Ranald Mackenzie and the US Army Fourth Cavalry as they journeyed across northwest Texas toward the High Plains and the defeat of the famous and feared Comanches.

As a kid some of us would occasionally ride our bicycles out to the monument to reread it and talk about it. Somewhere nearby, less than 100 years before, the Fourth Cavalry camped on their way to fight the Comanches. In a town where the biggest event was the coming of a Dairy Queen, this was momentous. Our place meant something. Something important, at least to us, had happened where we lived and somehow or another it gave our small-town lives significance. On the way home, riding bicycles as fast as we could, we reenacted the battles between the soldiers and the Comanches. Of course, none of us wanted to be the Comanches.

Faulkner famously said, "The past is not dead; it's not even past." Living in the early 1960s in that small west Texas town I was surrounded by the memories of the past. It seemed close enough that I could reach out and touch it, or at least listen to people face-to-face who could. My grandparents had not been alive at the close of the frontier. Indeed, neither were my great-grandparents, who were born in the decade after the removal of the Comanches and Kiowas to reservations in Oklahoma, but they had grown up dreading the nights with a full moon, known as a Comanche moon, for that's when the Comanches preferred to raid the scattered farms and

5

ranches. Stories of those fear-filled full-moon nights were passed along to their children and grandchildren. Even eighty or ninety years after the last Comanche had left the country, I didn't hear, "My, look at that beautiful full moon," from my grandparents, but "It's a Comanche moon," still carrying memories of the old dread.

On the nearby Clear Fork of the Brazos our family knew an old retired cowboy living in a decrepit cabin that had a den of rattlesnakes under the floor. Known to me by way of my grandfather as "Mister Bob," he was over eighty, wore a large Stetson and boots that came up to his knees with spurs, and he didn't pay the rattlesnakes any mind. Once asked by my uncle if he shot the rattlesnakes frequently found on his front porch, Mister Bob replied rather matter of factly, "No, I don't waste shells on rattlers. I just stomp 'em." Once Mister Bob rode his horse down to our campsite by the river and sat around the fire drinking scalding coffee. I was spellbound listening to his stories of cowboying before the turn of the century. There were times, he said, back during his youth when elderly Comanches would ride through the country looking for one last buffalo and remembering their own past back when West Texas belonged to them.

Years later, as a young Baptist preacher-in-the-making, I went to work for the Baptist Peace Fellowship of North America based in Atlanta. By this time, I was more interested in the racial issues of the Deep South, justice and peacemaking, the nuclear freeze movement, and working with the homeless. The dusty West Texas plains and memories of cowboys and Comanches were far away. We had a Peace Fellowship board meeting at the historic Koinonia Farm in South Georgia, the home of Clarence and Florence Jordan, radical Baptists who lived out the call of Jesus of justice and peace. Clarence had long passed, but Florence was still around and we spent half a day listening to her tell stories of Koinonia and the work of reconciliation. Later we went around the circle of board members introducing ourselves. Across the way was a short, barrel-chested black-haired man, an American Baptist pastor of a Native American church in Nebraska. He introduced himself as a full-blooded Comanche from Oklahoma, and as soon as I heard him say that, my hair stood up on end. When the introductions came to me, I said I was from West Texas and he snapped his head, staring at me. As soon as we had a break he made a bee-line to me. "So you're a Texan? From West Texas? You know that's Comanche country." No threat made or implied; just a simple statement of fact but made without a smile and to the point.

I turned red and my mouth was dry. "Yes, I know. Your ancestors and my ancestors were enemies." Here we were, two brothers in Christ, both Baptist preachers, but one Comanche and one Texan and the past, my past, his past, our past, had suddenly intruded into our present. Nervously, I made a motion with my hand of a snake wiggling through the grass, something I had heard as a boy. He nodded. "That's the sign of the Comanche. It's a snake." He smiled, "And it's also the sign of peace." And I smiled, breathing a little easier, "Yeah, I figure we could use some peace between us." He reached over and we embraced, and he said, "Let's go over and drink some iced tea and you tell me about how that Comanche country looks nowadays."

I swear that iced tea tasted like Communion wine.

Two Christianities

Kyle Childress

During a haircut my barber asked me, "Do you believe that zombies are real?" I said, "What?" not sure if I had heard her correctly. She asked again, "Do you believe that zombies are real?" Realizing that it was a serious question, I said, "No. Zombies are in movies, books, TV shows, and games. But they're not real."

She said, "My preacher says that zombies are real. He preaches that the devil reinvigorates dead bodies and that's where zombies come from."

Trying to avoid public criticism of another preacher I said, "Where in the Bible does he get this?"

She shot back, "Well, I don't know where he gets it. All I know is that he says we'd better get our guns ready because zombies are real."

"Where do you go to church?" I asked.

"I go to the Cowboy Church outside the loop. You know, you can see the rodeo arena out back."

"How many people attend on Sunday mornings to hear that zombies are real?"

She said, "Oh, we usually have somewhere around 400 on Sunday mornings, with most staying around Sunday afternoon for pot-luck dinner. We have roping, barrel-racing, and other rodeo events after that."

I didn't know whether to cry, cuss, or pray for mercy. Every Sunday I preach well-prepared, biblical sermons to a congregation of 80 to 100 people, while across town 400 people dress up as cowboys and pack into a church to hear that zombies are real and go rodeo afterwards.

Someone asked me the other day if I thought I was depressed; I thought about this barbershop conversation. I responded that the question is not *whether* I'm depressed. The question is why am I *not* depressed?

There was a huge headline in our local newspaper about the Texas controversy over US Army training code-named "Jade Helm" going on near Austin, Texas. Some conspiracy theorists were worried that the Obama Administration was secretly preparing for the Army to seize control of the Texas government, impose martial law (some say Sharia Law), and seize everyone's guns. Furthermore, apparently several Walmart stores had been inexplicably closed, which proved the point that the Army was preparing the stores to become detention centers for all those they arrested. Texas Governor Greg Abbot ordered the Texas State Guard to "observe" the Army training to make sure the Constitution was being observed.

The response by readers of the newspaper article was interesting. A few said that it was all true and we'd better get ready. A few others said it was extremism and how could anyone believe such weirdness and why did the paper even run the story. But most of the respondents said things like, "Well, you know where there's smoke there's fire. Sure, it's a nutty story but at the same time, I'm glad the governor is keeping an eye on the Army. Better to be safe than sorry." What was further disheartening is that many of those expressing such views are people I know in town who are active members of local churches.

I saw an ad for a new local food outlet that began with the words of Jesus to be prepared and "keep awake therefore, for you know neither the day nor the hour" (Matt 25:13). As I read on, I realized that this was an ad for a seminar on how to prepare for the coming end of the world. Besides learning how to grow your own food, there was training in guns and ammunition, making your home into a fort, and knowing the escape routes out of your community.

I feel like the character Walter Sobchak (played by John Goodman) in the movie *The Big Lebowski*, who screams, "Has the whole world gone crazy?!" Zombies? Secret Army takeover plots? Apocalypse?

One more item: As I write this, last week was the annual National Day of Prayer observance. Our local version is held at one of the city parks where everything is decorated in American flags, the community choir sings "God Bless America," and the series of speakers get up and fume, fuss, and shout over the demise of America, the dangerous rise of same-sex marriages, and why "Christians must take America back!" (Always an explanation point!) This year, like every year, it is an all-white audience completely distinct from our annual Martin Luther King Commemoration back in January. The pastors of the leading large white churches do not participate in the MLK events, but they always lead the NDP event. When invited to the MLK service, they often reply, "That's too radical." Yet, when some of us do not attend the NDP service, we hear, "Why can't the church be one? You folks don't want to be the unified church."

Which reminds me of Jesus' high priestly prayer in John 17, where he prays, "Holy Father, protect them in your name that you have given me, so that they may be one, as we are one" (John 17:11). For a long time, this has been my most discouraging word from Jesus. Is this what Jesus is praying? That I be unified with churches preaching about zombies, while getting our guns ready, waving the flag, and building bunkers?

I can't do this.

What I can do is trust that Jesus is praying for me, and for the wider church, when I can't. And while I do not think Jesus is talking about being one with gun-toting, flag-waving zombie fighters, I do think Jesus is calling us to humbly trust him as we learn to be one with others who come to Jesus's table or altar with hands that are empty, with hearts that are ready, and an appetite that hungers and thirsts for Jesus and his righteousness. In turn, formed and fed by Jesus we go out with the same humbling trust to serve the least of these.

Come quickly, Lord Jesus.

Old Pickups and Advent

Kyle Childress

There's an old joke I've told many times at prayer breakfasts in the basements of small town and rural churches among men with sunburned faces.

Seems this midwestern farmer was driving his few dairy cows across the road when a big Cadillac with long steer horns across the front bumper roared up and stopped in the road.

Behind the wheel was a fellow in a big cowboy hat. He watched the farmer with the cows and asked him, "This your farm?"

"Yep."

"How big a place you have here?"

The farmer motioned. "My property line runs from that line of trees you see over yonder to that ridgeline you see over there."

"Yeah, I have me a place down in Texas," the fellow in the big hat said. "I go out in the morning at sunup and get in my pickup and drive all day, and by the time the sun goes down, I still haven't reached my property line."

"Yep, I used to have a pickup like that," the farmer said.

Well, I have a pickup like that now. It's a 1977 Ford F-100 I inherited from my grandfather by way of my uncle and then my brother, who brought it to me the summer before last.

When my brother and I opened the cab door the first time, I quickly noticed the faint aroma of snuff that my grandfather dipped for nearly seventy years. The flashlight he always kept under the dashboard was in its place, and bolted over the back window was the same old gun rack he removed from and reinstalled in the various pickups he owned, more to hang hats and caps from than guns. Many of my earliest memories are of being in one pickup or another with him; he drove nothing else.

This one was his last. Old enough to be ugly but not old enough to be a classic, it has no frills, no air conditioner, no power steering, and a three-speed standard transmission that shifts on the steering column. It is not a comfortable pickup; it's a pickup for work.

In the bed is my grandfather's big toolbox. When I opened it, I discovered many of his tools, not only for his work as the all-purpose maintenance man at our local hospital for forty-four years, but also for working on the truck: a roll of duct tape, a hydraulic jack, a four-way lug wrench, extra bottles of motor oil, an extra radiator hose, an extra fan belt, jumper cables, various wrenches, screwdrivers, and a socket set. Here are the essentials for a man who knew how to work on his own truck.

There's an old truism among drivers of old pickups that goes something like this: You either drive a truck with everything working or you have a broke-down truck that needs work.

Wrong. Old trucks are driven *and* need working on at the same time. They are always in need of more work, but you get them going and are prepared for a breakdown wherever you go.

This is exactly why I've named my truck Habakkuk, for verse 2:3, which says, "If it seems slow, wait for it. It will surely come." And it is also why I'm learning patience by driving it. I'm learning that it takes a while to get somewhere, both because the truck is slow and because there is the likely chance that I'll need to pull over and open the hood and work on it somewhere along the way.

I'm no mechanic, but I'm learning. And that's why I have my friendly shade-tree garage on speed-dial and know the tow truck driver by his first name. Sometimes I can do the work myself, but most of the time it is beyond me and I need help. But as much as I love this truck, I get tired of working on it all the time. I get impatient that it takes longer than I expect to get someplace and that I need to be open to disruptions and breakdowns.

I'm no mechanic, but I am a pastor. And at this time of year, I see much more in this truck than a cantankerous old vehicle and memories of the grandfather I loved. I wonder, is my pickup preparing me for Advent?

This will be my twenty-fourth Advent with my present congregation. Twenty-four years of preaching these same Advent themes of waiting and preparing and patient endurance. After twenty-four years, I get tired of these same old texts and wonder what I'm going to say this time.

And after all these years, I wonder why my congregation still struggles with the same old things. After all, if I preach something, shouldn't they go out and practice it? After twenty-four years, shouldn't they be further down the road than they are?

O Lord, how long?

But I'm learning. Congregations always need work. And congregations never get to the place where they are "fixed" and running smoothly —at least none that I know. There's always something.

If it seems slow, wait for it. It will surely come.

The old teaching of the church is that if we pray for patience, God doesn't answer our prayer by miraculously turning us into patient people. Instead, God sends us opportunities to practice patience.

So God made me a pastor. And my grandfather left me an old pickup.

Porching, Friendship, and Ministry

Kyle Childress

A few years ago, when Jane (my wife) and the girls and I were away all summer on sabbatical, members of our church decided to build us a porch. They knew I loved porch sitting, and since our house did not have a porch, they thought it was a great idea to give us one. We agreed.

Since then, our porch has become the major gathering place for any social occasion at our house, none more so than the churchwide Easter potluck, with kids and adults everywhere, food, laughter, a slamming screen door ("You kids make up your minds—either in or out!"), and lots of conversation and stories among everyone lazily rocking back and forth in the rocking chairs and swing.

We all love the porch.

From time to time, I'll get a phone call from someone saying, "Are you going to be on your porch this evening?" To which I'll reply, "Yeah, I'll be there. Probably be out about seven."

Sure enough, around seven the caller will come walking up and join me on the porch. We'll visit, catch up on news, likely I'll tell a story or two, and eventually the visitor will get to whatever it is that's bothering him or her. We're not in a hurry; it is porching, after all.

What I've learned is that conversation on the porch is important ministry. If the caller comes to my study at the church for an appointment, it is called "counseling." But if someone drops by my porch and we sit in the rocking chairs, it is just two friends having a conversation. We're visiting.

Both counseling and visiting are significant ministries, but they are different. Part of the difference is need—sometimes the formality of the church building is more appropriate. But sometimes the difference has to do with different visions of the church and the role of the pastor.

The standard and dominant view is that the office of pastor has clearly defined boundaries and roles. For example, I was trained both in seminary and in college that the pastor should never make friends within the congregation. Having friends, in this view, is fraught with peril at every turn: the dangers of showing favoritism or having cliques within the church, the temptation to break confidences, the undermining of pastoral authority, and so on.

I was taught that the pastor's friendship is with God, and the rest of the church is on their own. I was taught that relationships of mutuality are different from those of service as a pastor, and that ordination creates a holy distance between the pastor and the people.

Maybe so. But maybe not.

What if the church is understood to be a community of friends? And what if the pastor is one of those friends? What if the hierarchy of the church is not as pronounced and formal as we might think? Perhaps the church is more like the body of Christ, with the different members connected to one another in Christ, but with each member having certain spiritual gifts, pastoring being one of those gifts.

I realize that I'm talking about two versions of the role of the pastor and models of the church in church teaching: Reformed and Anabaptist. But my Baptist polity has long mixed those two contrasting perspectives.

In practice, a new pastor has to earn her or his pastoral credibility within the first year or so. A congregation wants to see whether the pastor visits and cares and shows up. Do you listen to the people, and are you accessible?

They'll know whether you can lead worship and preach from the day they voted to call you. But will you be their pastor? That's a question that is answered over time. Beneath the issues of how well you visit and do pastoral care is the question of spiritual gifts. Are you a member of the body of Christ with the gift of being a pastor or not? In that first year, the congregation is discerning your calling and gifts.

But what does all that have to do with friendship and porches? In John 15:12–17, Jesus calls the church a community of friends who love one another. To me, the primary responsibility of a pastor is the nurturing and growing of such a community of mutual love. And that includes the pastor. We're in it, too. We're not separate or distanced from this community of friends. We're immersed in it; we participate in it. I believe we call it incarnation.

The pastor's authority comes out of this mutual love and friendship, not in spite of it. Over time, the members of the congregation come to know the pastor as a friend—a friend who prays for them, loves them, cares for them, shows up and works alongside them, and listens to them, while also being a friend who is immersed in God.

When Sunday morning rolls around, the twenty minutes of preaching comes out of this mutual friendship, of listening to the people and to God. My authority comes from being a friend who sometimes shares a strong word of challenge, and other times, a word of comfort in the midst of heartbreaking grief. They listen, not because I hold an office, but because we love one another and they recognize the gift and work of the Spirit in and through me. That's why they come and visit on my porch.

Cultural critic and writer bell hooks says, "In the days of my girlhood, when everyone sat on their porches, usually on their swings, it was the way we all became acquainted with one another, the way we created community."

She goes on: "A perfect porch is a place where the soul can rest."[1]

That sounds right to me. Sitting on my porch among friends, our souls can rest.

1. hooks, *Belonging*, 147, 152.

Truth Dazzles Gradually

Kyle Childress

At age fifty-one, Noah Adams, a host on National Public Radio, abruptly decided he had to have a piano so he invested in a new Steinway upright—a financial commitment that provided extra incentive to practice.

Adams tells this charming story of his first year of learning to play the piano in his book, *Piano Lessons: Music, Love, and True Adventures.* Yet learning to play was a daunting task, particularly given his already demanding schedule. He found it difficult and frustrating; he couldn't simply sit down and make the beautiful music he wanted. There were scales to learn, and basic rhythms to be mastered. Initially, he decided against going to a teacher, trying such shortcuts as a "Miracle Piano Teaching System" on the computer. A friend's warning proved to be prophetic: "You might be learning music with that computer, but you're not learning how to play."[1]

Eventually, Adams signed up for an intensive ten-day music camp. He discovered that there is no substitute for regular, disciplined practice and the tutelage of teachers. By the end of the first year, his frustrations began to recede. He actually desired time for practice. He had become initiated into the art of piano playing. He also learned to appreciate the craft of making and caring for pianos, as well as the importance of the history of pianos and great pianists—classical, jazz, blues, even rock-and-roll.

Some things take time. They can't be coerced and they can't be done quickly or easily. Besides playing the piano I think of gardening or learning to hit an inside curve-ball or reading poetry or learning to paint or dance. Raising children and being married is done over the long haul, too. I remember a comment by Wendell Berry who said that it takes more courage to be married day after day for fifty years than it does to be Samson. Samson

---

1. Adams, *Piano Lessons*, 86.

goes out and does one spectacularly faithful act while long marriages consist of thousands of small acts of fidelity over many years.

Knowing God takes time, too. God walked with his people for forty years across the wilderness, sat with his people for seventy years in exile, became a human being and pitched his tent with us for over thirty years before dying on a cross and then taking three days to be resurrected. To know this God means learning to walk alongside at the pace of God. When God called to Moses through the burning bush it was after Moses had been walking those desert hillsides for forty years. I'm convinced that those forty years were a kind of twelve-step recovery for Moses that freed him from his addiction to empire; it was not simply that it took forty years for Moses to be ready to lead the people out of imperial bondage, but it took forty years for Moses to be able to see the burning bush in the first place. For all I know, God had been burning bushes out there in the wilderness for a long time and Moses never had the eyes to see them or had failed to slow down enough to notice them.

The same goes for walking with Jesus. There is no substitute for the slow, sometimes painful growth that comes through disciplined habits of practice shaped by the crucified and risen Christ. One does not become an excellent piano player, painter, dancer, carpenter, or baseball player overnight; neither does one learn to become a Christian overnight. We can't know Jesus, the incarnate Son of God, in five quick easy lessons accompanied by an inspirational DVD. One needs teachers and mentors and a community of friends, and one needs to practice over a long period of time.

The first words spoken by Jesus in the Gospel according to John are, "What are you looking for?" (1:38). He is talking to two disciples of John the Baptist. And they respond in what sounds like a strange way, "Teacher, where are you staying?" What they are looking for, what they seek, is not so much information from the teacher; otherwise Jesus could have handed them his book or directed them to his website. No, they want to know him.

The word we translate as "staying" refers to the source of one's life and meaning. So when these two disciples ask Jesus, "Where are you staying?" they are asking, "What is it that sustains you? What power do you have? Where do you remain? Where do you live? How do you live? Who are you really?" It's the same word used in John later, over in chapter 15, when we are told we are to abide in Christ. Abiding, staying, remaining, residing, dwelling—they all take time.

Jesus says encouragingly, "Come and see." Then John tells us, "They came and saw where he was staying, and they remained with him that day." Here, in a simple and understated way, John gives us the essence of Christian discipleship. Discipleship is not primarily getting information or receiving the "right" answer; it is moving into the "house" with Jesus. It is living with Jesus Christ. And to live with Jesus takes time and community.

Emily Dickinson wrote, "Tell all the Truth but tell it slant— /... The Truth must dazzle gradually / Or every man be blind."[2] There are some things, and truth is one of them, that can be understood rightly only if we understand them over time. The very essence of truth is that it can only be known slowly, in bits and pieces that are chewed on, meditated on, reflected over, talked about, practiced and then practiced some more with others living with the same truth.

Gradually, as we come to know the truth of Jesus Christ, we may be dazzled.

2. Dickinson, *The Complete Poems of Emily Dickinson*, 506.

Out of the Old Rock

Kyle Childress

On the floor of the little church building where I served my first pastorate were three spots on the floor along the second pew where the varnish and polish were worn down to the bare wood. It was where Dude Templeton, Olga Blair, and Irene Calhoun rested their feet during the church service. These three women, three dear friends, sat on the same pew together every Sunday for forty years. Dude Templeton, who was in her mid-eighties about this time, had been sitting in the same place for forty-two years in a row without ever missing a Sunday.

I was a young and new pastor, but I knew what I was looking at as I gazed at the worn slick places on that floor. Fidelity.

Woody Allen had a point when he said that 90 percent of life consists in just showing up. I'm convinced that a large percentage of faith as a Christian consists in showing up. Dude Templeton, Ms. Blair, and Ms. Irene had been showing up every Sunday, usually twice, not to mention weddings and funerals and Wednesday night prayer meetings, for a long time.

Over its 125 years that church, like many in that part of Texas, had Baylor student pastors who served those churches for two or three years before going off to seminary or to a larger congregation somewhere. In that short time, these churches knew their calling was to train and teach these youngsters and prepare them for mature ministry. With profound patience, Dude, Ms. Blair, and Ms. Irene endured the enthusiasms of post-adolescent pastors, sat through the rock bands and revivals, gimmicks and creativity sometimes bordering on and other times crossing the line of the ridiculous. During the week this trio of elderly women quilted together and went down to the federally funded senior citizens center where they ate lunch in fellowship with other elders of the community. What all these seniors—white and black—enjoyed doing the most after the meal was sitting around the piano and singing hymns, reading and reciting Scripture to one another, and discovering friends for the first time in their octogenarian lives of another race who, surprise of surprises, were just as Christian, if not more so, than they were. At church suppers these three women were legends. Dude taught the younger women that in cooking for church suppers it was imperative to practice two things: cook your very best because it is for the Lord, and cook a lot because it is for the church. My testimony is that she knew how to do both.

Dude had been in church all of her eighty-five years and was raised just down the road. She had married a good, quiet man who farmed nearby. Between the two of them they had and raised ten kids during the Depression, World War II, droughts and hardship, and through it all, they never wavered. They never missed church—except for a couple of times when she was giving birth on a Sunday.

The first time she missed church after forty-two straight years was while I was her pastor and she had to go into the hospital to have her gall bladder removed. While the young doctor visited with her as she entered the hospital, he asked her, "When was the last time you've been in the hospital? She said, "I've never been in one." He asked a little indignantly, "Well, didn't you have any children?" She reared up in the bed, "I'll have you know that I've had ten kids but I didn't have to go to the hospital to have them! I had them at home!"

Dude Templeton and her friends were "out of the old rock." The phrase comes from the Texas writer, J. Frank Dobie, who used to say that the settlers of Texas, the pioneers were the "old rock." They were the ones with the tenacity and perseverance to settle this country and make a living, put down roots and raise families. Dobie said that then there were those who were "out of the old rock." He meant those who embodied the same determination, faithfulness, and long-haul perseverance exhibited by those who had gone before them. These three elder women were not settlers but close. It was not simply a matter that up into the 1940s Dude still had a dirt floor in her house or that she and her husband drove a wagon, and not a car, up into the 1950s. "Out of the old rock" means that Dude, like her friends, had that faithful steadiness, that sheer dogged devotion—to God, to her church, to her family, indeed, in everything in her life.

Fidelity.

The church has long known that we need to be people of fidelity over a long time and we need to train our young people in this way. Theologian Walter Brueggemann said, "The people of God were the sort of culture who loved their young enough to tell them what they had heard from God. They loved their young enough to say, 'you don't have to make up the way as you go. You don't have to reinvent the path to God on your own. We'll tell you. We'll show you the way.'"[1] And we'll point you to others who have been walking this way a long time and you can learn to walk with them.

Author Bill McKibben suggests that many of our generation have been good at many things, but tenacity or faithfulness is not one of them. Perhaps we are good at the novel and the innovative, and the good Lord knows I sought to be both when I was the young pastor in that rural church. But when we look at those who have gone before us, sometimes we can see that on most days, it's enough to be living faithfully together, adding another increment of quotidian devotion to God and each other, everyday faithfulness, giving one another the benefit of the doubt, being patient, and never, ever giving up.

A sign on the Winchester Cathedral in England says as you enter the church, "You are entering a conversation that began long before you were born and will continue long after you're dead."

One Sunday morning I watched young parents Bill and Tammy pass their six-week-old daughter Kara along the row to that trio of elder women. All three were born toward the end of the nineteenth century and here they were sweet-talking to a baby who would likely live well into the twenty-first. This was a conversation of fidelity that had begun a long time ago and by the grace of God would continue on.

---

1. Turner and Malambri, eds., *A Peculiar Prophet*, Kindle loc. 899. The quote from Brueggemann appears in a William Willimon sermon, "Surrounded by a Great Cloud of Witnesses."

Will Campbell, Reconciliation, and Us

Kyle Childress

From time to time we'll have a visitor in church, a family or an individual, who just fits in; they like being here and we like having them. I can tell it by watching them sing the hymns or how they interact with people after the service or sometimes by the nodding of their heads during my sermon. A church member might comment to me later in the week, "I had a good conversation with our visitor on Sunday and they seemed to be 'our kind of people.' We'll likely see them come back."

St. Augustine considers the church a gathering of friends. In church you meet friends you never knew you had, so I'm glad when someone visits and immediately discovers our church as friends they never knew they had. In our culture friendship is usually based upon affinity, so our friends are those with whom we share common interests and perspectives. For our church that usually means that we vote liberal Democrat, believe in inclusivity and diversity, and have at least a master's degree. Usually it means we care about some of the same things: environmental issues, backpacking or canoeing, and local foods. We usually drive a hybrid car and have high-achieving children, read books, listen to NPR, and enjoy a glass of wine with dinner. Biblically it means that we are comfortable with the basics of historical and social criticism. Theologically we're mostly in the middle or left of middle in the great scheme of orthodoxy and we like our preachers to have well-prepared and thoughtful homilies on Sunday morning. If you can check most of these on your own list when visiting you'll likely find a home with us.

But what if you're not "one of our kind of people"? What if you come from a different economic background and your formal education ended after high school and you went to work? What if instead of NPR you listen to country and prefer Bud to Beaujolais, drive a big-ass truck instead of a Prius, know how to break down a Remington 870 shotgun in the dark sitting in a duck blind in a cold rain, and have fixed more than one radiator hose with nothing more than duct-tape, a Case pocket knife, and the flame of a Bic lighter? And what if your theology is pretty much the Book, the Blood, and the Blessed Hope? But at the same time, perhaps our church ended up caring for your mother as she died or your daughter has found a home among the youth of our congregation and you find yourself visiting. Is there a place for you? Will you have any friends? Is this a church for all people or just for people of the same affinity group?

We live in a society that is increasingly polarized with the culture wars; we have blue and red states. Churches seem to be reflecting the same polarization and are organized less around doctrinal convictions and denominational loyalties and are becoming more Fox News churches and MSNBC churches or Republican churches and Democrat churches, educated class congregations and blue-collar working class ones, with churches based upon differences of race adding to the various divides.

Clarence Jordan used to point out that among Jesus' disciples in the Gospels were both Matthew the tax-collector and one called Simon the Zealot. We know nothing more about Simon except his identification, which means that he probably stood against and hated everything that Matthew the tax-collector stood and worked for. In the ancient Jewish world of Jesus' day there were no positions and identities more polarized than these. Yet both were among Jesus' twelve disciples. Clarence said that he figured that on more than one occasion Jesus had to sleep between the two around the campfire to keep one from sticking a knife between the ribs of the other. Yet this was the nature of discipleship with Jesus. Polar opposites called together to follow Jesus and having their differences transformed so that they both became more like the one they followed. This is what the Apostle Paul called the ministry of reconciliation (2 Cor 5:18). Here is the picture of the church based not upon affinity, but upon the reconciliation of Christ.

I've never known anyone more devoted to the ministry of reconciliation than Will Campbell. He started off as a young Southern Baptist from Mississippi committed to fighting the racism of his native South. Will learned the hard way to be ever careful about choosing up sides. God in Christ does not choose sides, but in dying makes us all whole. Our job is to join up with what Christ has accomplished: be reconciled!

Will worked hard at building reconciling friendships with the most unlikely of people. He was friends with black activists but also with white members of the Ku Klux Klan. This did not mean that Will had no critical words for the Klan; it meant that he spoke to them as a friend and reconciler.

In his book *And Also With You* Will tells the story of being in the deepest part of the Mississippi woods walking alongside Sam Bowers of the Ku Klux Klan and Kenneth Dean, long-time civil rights activist. Bowers is taking them to a secret gathering place of the Klan.

"Beside me was Bowers, a man alleged to have been responsible for multiple murders, bombings, and mayhem. On the other side of me was Ken Dean, a man who had risked his own life trying to save the lives of black citizens ... It was the greatest test of my tentative understanding of unconditional grace as overshadowing, overcoming, conquering humanity's inherent sinfulness I had ever known. The scandal of the gospel I had heard preachers and theologians talk about in generalities all my life assumed an even more outrageous posture. Is grace abounding here in this darkening arcane forest? Truly unconditional grace? Something as crazy as Golda Meir chasing Hitler around the pinnacles of heaven, and after a thousand years he stops and lets her pin a Star of David on his chest? Who said that?... I felt a strange oneness with the two men with me. And an even more unfamiliar concord with those I knew had convened on this ground to plan missions of atrocity."[1]

Church is not about finding "our kind of people." Rather church is learning how to have all kinds of people in the same congregation where together we are reconciled, become friends, and are transformed to be Christ's people.

No easy task, but nevertheless that's our calling.

1. Campbell, *And Also With You*, 264.

The Hood Abides

Kyle Childress

Twenty-five years ago some pastors shared a meal at a Baptist meeting full of division and fighting that made us desperate to be with friends. Soon our meal and conversation evolved into a quick overnight gathering, frantic with frozen pizza, cold beer, cigars, and talk into the wee hours. It didn't take long before we were doing the overnight thing twice a year; after Joe and Charlie came up with generous and beautiful ranch houses with plenty of room, owned by extended family members, we turned our get-together into a week and Nathan gave us the name "the Neighborhood" for Will Campbell's little radical band of friends in his novel *The Glad River*.

Six of us clergy friends meeting twice a year for a week for over twenty-five years—that's the Neighborhood, or the "Hood" for short. We block the dates on our calendars six months out and even our congregations do planning around them. We talk and plan and joke and anticipate with increasing excitement in the weeks approaching our little gathering while tending to myriad pastoral tasks so the Hood will be worry-free over what we've left undone back home. We bring books and sermon materials (Hood or no Hood a sermon still awaits us when we get home), and movies. We love our movies. Or to be more exact, we love a particular movie: *The Big Lebowski*.

We drive, fly, speed, shop for groceries and whatever else we need to do in order to be at the Hood by Monday evening. Rushed and tired from rushing, still on full-speed-ahead-time, we are excited and full of adrenaline; though we are glad to be away from the frantic stressors behind us, the habits of speed are still with us. We are committed to slowing down but it takes a while and it takes intention. The poet Theodore Roethke said, "I wake to sleep, and take my waking slow"; that's us as we move into Hood time on Tuesday morning. Slowly we get to our coffee and the first order of business that sets the tone for the rest of our week of learning to abide —living into hanging out; learning simply to be. With coffee in hand we sit down and watch *The Big Lebowski*, the Coen Brothers comedy about the Dude, of whom narrator Sam Elliot says, "he's a lazy man—and the Dude was most certainly that. Quite possibly the laziest in all of Los Angeles County, which would place him high in the runnin' for laziest worldwide." After fifteen years of watching the movie twice a year we've all memorized the script, favorite lines are repeated to one another throughout the year, and obscure references show up in our emails and conversation. The Dude has become a kind of hero or saint to us. He shows us the way.

Every one of us is amused that the Dude is the patron saint of the Hood. In our various ways and contexts, we are now or have been driven pastors in thriving churches and ministries with much going on. To enjoy to the point of cult status a movie character known for underachieving slacking, whose preferred dress is pajamas and a bathrobe, and who will blow an evening lying in the bathtub, getting high and listening to an audiotape of whale songs, is ironic, to say the least. In a kind of summary of who he is at the end of the movie the Dude says, "Yeah man. Well, you know, the Dude abides."

Abiding is not something that comes to mind when thinking about our modern lives or even our church's lives. We not only do not abide, we don't even know what it is anymore. "Get 'er done" is more our motto. Church members are working longer hours or perhaps working two jobs, while also running kids to their numerous after-school activities, and we clergy are frantically fighting to find ways for them to worship God and to serve others. Even when I go to our local ministerial alliance the most common response to "How are you?" is "Busy."

For us and for our churches, the old social activist saying, "If not us, who? And if not now, when?" echoes in our heads. With concealed racism rampant and unconcealed sexism on the rise, impoverishment, climate change, injustice, plus church members with cancer and heart disease and all of the rest, someone's got to do something!

But "abide" keeps whispering to us. Not just from the Dude, but more, from Jesus himself (didn't Jesus go around in a robe, too?). Jesus says that in order to know God, know love, and be able to do the specific work of this loving God, we have to abide in him. Simply being—being together in Christ is essential, not an addendum (John 15). When someone used to ask

Will Campbell what we are to do in a world going to hell in a hand-basket, he'd say, "Do? Do nothing! Be something! Be what you are—reconciled to God and humanity." And he'd quote Bonhoeffer, who pointed out that it was an "Anglo-Saxon failing" to imagine that the church was supposed to have a ready answer for every social problem. Will's friend, and another patron saint of ours (and another guy in a robe), Thomas Merton, said, "Before you do a damned thing, just be what you say you are, a Christian; then no one will have to tell you what to do. You'll know."[1]

After four days of sitting on the porch and watching cows graze, telling stories, and reading books, going for walks and just hanging out, we point ourselves toward home and the work of ministry which awaits us. Every gathering, twice a year for twenty-five years, we end our Neighborhood in a circle, arms around each other, and someone prays. We are grateful. God's grace is sufficient. The Hood abides.

1. Quoted in Campbell, *Up to Our Steeples in Politics*, 152 –53.

I'm a Preacher

Rodney Wallace Kennedy

Will Campbell often said he was a preacher. That has always been good enough for me. Minister, pastor, rector, father—the list of names for clergy seem endless—but preacher works for me. I am a preacher and a teacher of preachers. The teaching of preaching saddens and gladdens my heart. It is ecstasy and agony. The sadness comes from how preaching has been demoted to the back of the curriculum and MDiv graduates are sent out to face congregations armed with one course in the introduction to preaching. Along with allowing students to graduate without sniffing a Greek New Testament or a Hebrew Bible, the insufficient attention paid to preaching galls me.

What gladdens my heart are my students. When they struggle to understand the rich rhetorical theory that is the burden of David Buttrick's magisterial textbook, *Homiletic*, I smile. Preaching ought to be a struggle and never be about being flip, comfortable, cute, or nice. When my students resist the gigantic reading lists that I impose on them, they wince and I insist they start now with the habit of being life-long readers. If law school is supposed to teach you to think, seminary should teach you to read. As Stanley Hauerwas reminds us, what we learned to do in seminary was read. He adds, "I like to think that seminaries might be best understood as schools of rhetoric."[1]

Not all my students are convinced that reading matters as much as I claim. One student, a semester after making an "A" in my class, saw me at an event. He hustled over to greet me and said, "Dr. Kennedy, I like what you said about reading. I want you to know I have read a book this year." It was September!

1. Hauerwas, *Working with Words*, 86–87.

Stanley Hauerwas, in a commencement address at Eastern Mennonite Seminary, argues that seminary is meant to prepare you to spend a
life reading. "You must continue to read and study even though you may
receive little reward for doing so."[2] Whenever you are tempted to do mind-
less ministerial chores, get another great big book and read some more.

One time I read that the average rabbi reads six times more books per
year than the average Protestant preacher. My competitive juices shifted
into overdrive and I decided to do something about that. The rabbi at Temple Israel, David Sofian, turns out to be a voracious reader and has become
my best friend. We push one another and it has been a blessing. We are
currently arguing about the meaning of holiness and writing a book about
it. When we need to have fun, we invite our Episcopal priest friend, Jack
Koepke, to join us at the Wine Gallery and we do stand-up comedy. Our act
is called "A Rabbi, A Priest, and A Preacher Walk into a Bar." You wouldn't
believe the amount of reading required to prepare a fifteen-minute comedy
skit.

Preachers are the last generalists on the planet. That means our reading lists require us to sit, hat in hand, before all the other disciplines. A
preaching professor once told me that I should be reading six books from
six different disciplines at all times. The year was 1978 and I took him literally, because in 1978 I took everything literally. Hell, I even still read news-
papers—*The Washington Post, The New York Times, The Wall Street Journal,*
and *The Dayton Daily News.*

As a preacher, the most helpful genre of reading is novels and short
stories, especially short stories by Southern writers. Reynolds Price claims
that the novel comes closer to being a truly Christian form. In its attempt to
elicit understanding of and mercy for all creation, the novel teaches mercy
and forgiveness for all creation. As Allan Gurganus puts it, "There are those
who believe that the sermon is the primary literary form of American life.
From Cotton Mather's surreal visions of hell to Hawthorne's allegories of
American guilt, to Whitman's promissory hymns, to Twain's biting moral-
izing satires, to Dreiser's Aschcan School of Social Darwinism, to Faulkner's
postlapsarian South, to Flannery O'Connor's godless modernity vs. ancient
mysteries, to Marilynne Robinson's watery, postmodern version of heaven
and hell in *Housekeeping,* we feel the sermon's lash and balm in every great
American book."[3] It is this connection between fiction and preaching that

2. Ibid., 87.

3. Quoted in Ketchin, *The Christ-Haunted Landscape,* Kindle ed., loc. 5354–55.

led me to the practice of having my homiletics students read a short story for every class during the semester. I hold up the story as the form the sermon takes.[4] When our sermons can be compared to the parables of Jesus, we will know that we are touching the hem of the garment of the greatest preaching possible.

Preachers are apprenticed to reading. Only by reading are we able to train our minds to receive the word that may come from God. Harry Crews, Southern novelist, said that he got his practice of sitting at the typewriter every day for three hours from Flannery O'Connor. He speaks of what we write as a mystery, knowing that we can't explain where we get the stuff we write. Crews quotes O'Connor: "I go to the typewriter every day for three hours so if anything comes, I am prepared to receive it."[5]

Pat Conroy's *My Reading Life* inspires my own reading to this moment. He also taught me that the best writers/preachers have larcenous skills. I try to teach my students to at least steal good material and to have enough preaching sense to know good material from so-so stuff.

Pat Conroy says, "Because I was raised Roman Catholic, I never feared taking any unchaperoned walks through the fields of language. Words lifted me up and filled me with pleasure. I've never met a word I was afraid of, just ones that left me indifferent or that I knew I wouldn't ever put to use. When reading a book, I'll encounter words that please me, goad me into action, make me want to sing a song. I dislike pretentious words, those highfaluting ones with a trust fund and an Ivy League education. Often they were stillborn in the minds of academics, critics, scientists. They have a tendency to flash their warning lights in the middle of a good sentence."[6]

I work hard to turn my students into word sleuths. A few more nuggets from Conroy: "I could build a castle from the words I steal from books I cherish." "I hunt down words that have my initials branded on their flanks." "Words call out my name when I need them to make something worthy out of language."[7]

Working with words is a long, patient apprenticeship and preachers have the privilege of serving them. And the place words hang out are in the hundreds of books you are reading and will read. So when I ask you, "What are you reading," I am not making small talk. I'm asking you the

4. Ketchin, *The Christ-Haunted Landscape*, 394.

5. Ibid., 339.

6. Conroy, *My Reading Life*, 86.

7. Ibid., 87.

WILL CAMPBELL, PREACHER MAN

most significant question in the world. I have a Pat Conroy saying printed and sitting on my desk: "To be boring is not just a sin; it's a crime."[8]

8. Ibid., 42. Conroy reports that the saying is from his high school English teacher, Gene Norris.

Preaching Is a Sacrament

Rodney Wallace Kennedy

I will stand at my watch-post,
and station myself on the rampart;
I will keep watch to see what he will say to me,
and what he will answer concerning my complaint.
Then the Lord answered me and said:
Write the vision;
make it plain on tablets,
so that a runner may read it.
For there is still a vision for the appointed time;
it speaks of the end, and does not lie.
If it seems to tarry, wait for it;
it will surely come, it will not delay (Hab 2:1–3).

I have been standing at the watch-post of preaching for my entire life. Hat in hand before an array of scholars and disciplines, I have devoted my life to preaching. Student, practitioner, and teacher—I self-identify as a preacher. "Write the vision" is my constant task and whether or not the words I have received are from God remains to be determined. And the sermon must come without delay because Sunday waits for no preacher. Whether treasure or trash, prepared or not, on Sunday we must speak a word to the people. As Doris Betts said about the work of the ministry: "It is terribly hard; I don't know how they do it."[1]

Preachers are supposed to have an iconic relationship with the Bible. There is a lot of talking about the Bible among preachers, but I find it ironic that some Baptists are known as the people of the Book and are always going

---

1. Quoted in Ramsey, Jr., *Preachers As Misfits, Prophets, and Thieves,* Kindle ed., loc. 170.

on about the infallible, inerrant Word of God. Yet most Baptists read very little Scripture in Sunday worship. Episcopalians, and other churches that use the lectionary, on the other hand, dispense large portions of Scripture every Sunday in faithfulness to the belief that the words of Scripture are "some molten words perfected in an oven seven times."[2] A Baptist preacher can take half a verse and preach for forty-five minutes; an Episcopal priest can take four readings and seventy-five verses and preach for eight minutes.

I'm often called by my fellow Baptists a Catholic Baptist. There's a small group of Baptists—mostly university and seminary professors—that make up this unique group. We have authored a book that makes the case for weekly observance of the sacrament, the use of creeds, the full observance of the Christian year, and the liturgy of *The Book of Common Prayer*. Among Baptists, it has not been a hot sell. My ecclesiology is a potentially unstable mixture of Anabaptist and Anglican doctrines of the church. I have combined "holiness" and witness as the characteristics of the whole church and I have assumed that the sacraments and an episcopal order give the church its common identity across time and space.

Two Baptists have deeply influenced this odd mixture. Will Campbell, who famously defined the gospel as "We are all bastards and God loves us anyway," is the Anabaptist, Mennonite influence in my life. Will left the high church steeples after being a pastor for only three years. He served as chaplain at Ole Miss when the school was first integrated. One of his best books, *And Also with You*, is about Duncan Gray, an Episcopal priest/bishop that Will loved as his brother. He ended as a radical Anabaptist—a pacifist, a faithful witness. His novel, *Glad River*, is about a Mississippi boy who tells his mama that he will not be baptized until he finds a real Baptist. His "Baptist" turns out to be a Cajun Catholic from the bayous of Louisiana. His baptism takes place in a secluded pool fed by a majestic waterfall. Nestled among the cypress trees there is a tall cypress knee that looks for all the world like the Virgin Mary. When a character called Model T first discovered the virgin, he placed a necklace around her neck with a silver dollar attached. He tells Kingston and Doops that no one else has ever laid eyes on the Virgin. He knows this because, as he puts it, "Now, if somebody else had been here, anybody, one of two things would have happened. Either they would have cut it down with a crosscut saw and hauled it out of this swamp by sundown, or else they would have slapped a concrete road where that

2. Osherow, *Dead Men's Praise*, 53.

34

bayou is and they'd be charging folks a dollar a head just to come here and see it. Man, believe me, this place would be a shrine by now."

Doops wonders what would have happened if a Baptist had found the silver dollar. "They would have grabbed my dollar," Model T said.[3]

My other Baptist brother was John Claypool. John wandered in the wilderness that is the Southern Baptist Convention for years attempting to convince those Gnostics who practiced the "real absence of Jesus" because they were afraid of the incarnation and the "real presence of Jesus," that he was a sacramental Baptist. John eventually came home to the Episcopal Church.

I am proposing that preaching is a sacrament based on my reading of John 6. If preaching is granted sacramental status, as John 6 may propose, then the elements of the sacrament are words. Jesus the Bread of Life is also the Word. The words we read and speak and the speech acts we enact are the bread and wine. We are the world's Eucharist. "You give them something to eat," Jesus said to the apostles. As those who stand in that apostolic line, it remains our primary task to give them something to eat and drink —word and table. As Flannery O'Connor said, "If [the sacrament] is just a symbol, then to hell with it."[4]

To concentrate on the word in a world where words seem bankrupt, in a church where even one of our leading homiletics professors, Richard Lischner, laments that we have reached the end of words,[5] how can we bring a word from the Lord? Isn't our temptation to go with the cultural cupcake offering on Sunday morning—fluffy, savvy, slick, easy words? It is no easy thing to make the word be for the congregation the presence of the living Christ. As Barbara Brown Taylor remarks, "The problem, for a preacher, is how to call people to the table with the language at hand, especially when so many of them have become suspicious if not downright disdainful of the spoken word. It is a problem that is compounded by God's own silence."[6] Yet most people seemed convinced that any old stick can throw together a sermon and speak for twelve minutes about something on a Sunday. Plato, lamenting the fake rhetoric and florid speeches of his day, compared the making of a speech to cooking and called it a knack in *Phaedrus*. All one needs is a small flame and a recipe. Then like cutting out cookies in

3. Campbell, *The Glad River*, Kindle ed., loc. 3531.
4. O'Connor, *The Habit of Being*, 125.
5. Lischer, *The End of Words*, 6.
6. Taylor, *When God Is Silent*, xi.

elaborate designs, out pops a well-done sermon with vanilla icing. It's a knack. And it gets us by. A preacher once told me that he had four years' worth of sermons and he could stay anywhere for eight years. I questioned his math and he said, "I preach my sermons for four years and then next four years I preach them backwards."

If we can lay aside our assumptions about the greatness and grandness of our preaching ability, we might learn to be a bit more creative, more innovative, and more imaginative. I have learned much about preaching from sources unrelated to the seminary or the church and I learned it from novelists and poets. Reynolds Price insists that our task is to give the world as much mercy as possible. As a sacrament, preaching has the ability to offer mercy—the outward sign of the inward business of the church.

Doris Betts has a short story, "This Is the Only Time I'll Tell It," which contains that highest vision of what it means for a church to take seriously the vows of infant baptism. A baby is rescued from drowning at the hands of her drunken father and the little congregation gives the baby to the single woman who saved the child's life. The narrator's description of the baptism never fails to move me: "We formed a wheel of people near Zelene's wood-pile for a baptism with cold water dipped out of the spring. The preacher bent, whispered to her, waited, poured a cupped handful on the head which now belonged to Silver Bolick."[7] For the next fifteen years, the church members took their turns helping raise Silver and thus keep all the promises made by the congregation at her baptism. Now, this is an enacted sermon. Here is the crossroads between word and action.

We are too casual by three times about our relationship to preaching. Carlyle Marney taught me that nothing is so devastating to love as a casual approach when passion is expected. By and large, we preach as if nothing were at stake. Marney said, "God must have a great compassion to watch a man suffering from an exhaustion he does not recognize acting-out all sorts of frustrations in a pulpit!"[8] We all do this. There can be no casual preaching, no merely functional sermon. All the sermons in a church year ought to offer the prospect of a word from the Lord—a chance to say a Yes or No that matters. "God is whoever raised Jesus from the dead, having before raised Israel from Egypt," says Robert Jenson in *Systematic Theology*.[9] There

---

7. Betts, "This Is the Only Time I'll Tell It," in Ketchin, *The Christ-Haunted Landscape*, Kindle ed., loc. 3230–3316.

8. Marney, "A Come-and-Go-Affair," in ed. Cox, *The Twentieth Century Pulpit*, 138.

9. Quoted in Hauerwas, *Working with Words*, 79.

is no casual response to that. On the night in which he was betrayed, our Lord said, "Take, eat, this is my body." There is no casual response to that.

The job no one wants, the job no one thinks exists, words that disappear in thin air—of such is vocation of the preacher. Our task is made even more difficult because we also don't really know what we are supposed to say. Given the frivolous nature of American politics, for example, a preacher takes life in hand to even read the parable of the Good Samaritan, Matthew 25, or the text Jesus used for his first sermon. I have congregants accuse me of promoting left-wing Democratic politics simply because I read the lesson appointed for the day. What should bother them at this point is that on their own they have connected the Gospel to what they assume are left-wing politics.

And how in the name of all that is sacred are we supposed to kayak our way through the turbulent currents of American politics? My general rule of thumb is that as long as there are both Democrats and Republicans mad at something I have preached, I am probably close to the gospel.

Sure, there is much in our preaching that represents our opinion, but at least it is an ordained opinion. People will say to me, "Preacher, that's just your opinion." "That may be so," I respond, "but it is ordained opinion." In the movie *Metropolitan*, a character defended his obtuseness by saying, "Just because you haven't read a book, doesn't mean you can't have an opinion on it. I haven't read the Bible, but I have an opinion on it." That character has many disciples populating our churches every Sunday morning.

Church members often complain that our sermons are meddling in politics. Since we are charged to interpret the secular world through the words of Scripture, we are not politicians; we are theologians. As soon as we read the health care policy of the Good Samaritan, we are, as Will Campbell put it, "up to our steeples in politics." Matthew 25 dares to say that our eternal destiny is related to "for I was hungry and you gave me food, I was thirsty and you gave me something to drink, I was a stranger and you welcomed me, I was naked and you gave me clothing, I was sick and you took care of me, I was in prison and you visited me."

In spite of these and many other complex challenges, I remained convinced that preaching is a good the whole people of God have in common and I believe that preaching is a sacrament. We don't have enough sacraments because we don't have a strong enough sacramental imagination and we are handicapped by seeing the secular world in which we live as a threat rather than an opportunity.

Like Habakkuk, our task is to stand, watch, and speak with reticence and humility as much mercy as we can muster. I believe that the goal of preaching is to give all of creation mercy. Of such is the uncertain but glorious nature of the sacrament of preaching. I am a preacher—God, yes.

A Truth Serum?

Rodney Wallace Kennedy

A former Southern Baptist spokesperson has been talking about a "truth serum." I am not quite sure how the truth serum metaphor works, but it appears to be a metaphor for whether or not a person accepts a particular understanding of biblical authority. The truth serum, when administered properly, by an authorized technician of the Authority of the Bible staff, will reveal whether the person injected is a true evangelical or a faux evangelical.

Truth serum usually indicates that someone has been captured and injected with a psychoactive medication to obtain information from subjects who are unwilling to provide it otherwise. For example, the KGB used truth serum during the Cold War. One of their operatives reported, "The 'remedy which loosens the tongue' has no taste, no smell, no color, and no immediate side effects. And, most important, a person has no recollection of having the 'heart-to-heart talk'" and felt afterwards as if they suddenly fell asleep.

Do you get Kool-Aid with the truth serum? When the Authority of the Bible team kidnaps a person do they take them to an underground bunker and torture them before administering the truth serum? This is so clandestine.

I dreamed I was captured by the Authority. A pair of men grabbed me off the sidewalk in front of First Baptist Dayton, on West Monument Avenue, in broad daylight. They knocked me out, threw a black bag over my head and took me to a secret location.

When I regained consciousness, someone gave me a shot. Then another person started asking me questions:

Do you believe in the authority of the Bible? "I believe in the authority of God the Father, the Son, and the Holy Spirit and her church. I believe in the authority of persuasion."

Do you believe the Bible is inerrant? "Of course not. That is an impossible truth claim. No original copy of the Bible exists, and there are problems with all the translations."

Do you support gay marriage? "Yes."

Do you believe Adam was the first, original man? "No."

Do you believe the world was created in six, literal, actual days? "No."

My tongue, now loosened by the truth serum, just went off. "I also believe in the politics of Jesus: peace and caring for the poor. I believe in loving my enemies and in evolution and I don't believe there is a literal hell. I think the church cannot gather in the true sense on Sunday morning because we have not resolved the race issue in America. I don't believe America is God's country or that patriotism is a Christian virtue. When I drink beer, I drink to the glory of God!"

I must have passed the test, because the two guys that kidnapped me put me back in the van, put the black hood over my head, and deposited me in front of First Baptist Dayton, on West Monument Avenue.

Since I don't remember any of this happening, I'm sure it was a dream. After all, I tell the truth and there's no need to give me a truth serum. Peace!

God Is Not Scary

Rodney Wallace Kennedy

American Christianity is filled with preaching that tells us all the time that we will perish at the hands of a vindictive, punitive God. These preachers have no room in their theology for those majestic words of a scared Jacob: "and yet my life is preserved." God never runs out of "yet."

Of course we should "fear" God, but that is a liturgical term and refers to reverence. I am talking about a deep gut-level fear. Do we have a scary God? There are plenty of scary texts in the Bible. Do you think that if we ignore some Scripture that we don't have to deal with it? Look, I think we have to deal with all of it. There's not a text that we can afford to overlook. We have to pore over, read slowly, and interpret as faithfully as possible. But we live in a church culture where one part of the Christian world is scared to death of God and the other part treats God like the guy sitting next to them at the bar having a glass of pinot noir.

I would mark it as a life-defining moment, when a person discovers that she doesn't have to be afraid of God. When the truth dawns that God is good, God is love, God is merciful, God is long-suffering, God is not out to do us in but win us over, God is not the grand enforcer but divine encourager, I believe that is a deeply moving spiritual experience.

We don't have a scary God, but some of God's people are scary people, and some give all they have to making God sound as scary as possible. There are all the preachers with their doom and gloom messages. The newest *Left Behind* movie stars Nicolas Cage. There is not a shred of truth in any of the rapture theology. It is a fear and damnation doctrine concocted from a Scottish teenage girl's dream by a separatist Anglican named Darby. It is a misreading of New Testament passages that are talking about resurrection. The rapture teaches that God is going to save Israel from the forces of the

41

anti-Christ and then Jesus is going to morph into a supernatural Hitler and commit genocide against all the unbelieving Jews. This is a scary teaching. The rapture teaches that Jesus is coming back to destroy creation and kill all the humans who have not trusted in his name. It is a scary doctrine that instead of praying for the peace of Israel, prays for war in the Middle East to trigger the rapture. There are rapture believers exulting and rejoicing over the current conflict in Gaza. It can only mean the rapture is coming soon! These rapture lovers have been predicting the end of the world again and again and again and every time, every time, every time, the announced date has been wrong. These Christians are no doubt sincere, but they are 100 percent wrong, wrong, wrong. This gnostic-based escape plan has no relationship to the love of God for all of creation. We don't have a scary God; we have scary teaching.

Then there all those scary Christians shouting that we are going to hell if we don't vote right, oppose practically everything, and stand up for Jesus and his literal Bible. The web is filled with the vitriol of these well-meaning Christians. It is their default setting when you disagree with them: You are of the devil and you are going to hell. Teach or preach anything that goes against the will of Right-wing Christianity in America and somebody will consign you to hell—body, soul, and spirit. Put this down: It is not God who is angry; it is the people who claim to be such wonderful Christians. Why are Christians foot-stomping, temper-tantrum throwing mad? I can't find it anywhere in the Bible where God says, "Go and be angry at everybody about everything." It says "Go and make disciples."

In the midst of a scared people with some really scary messages riddled with bad news, threats of violence and hell, here is an alternative to the bad news being preached in America. God is not out to scare us but to give us life. Doug Frank, in his insightful book, *A Gentler God*, appeals to all the Christians who have been hurt by the religion of the scary God, and at times I had to put down the book and weep and touch the scars that I still have from the message of the almighty punishing, threatening God, to trust in the good news about God delivered by Jesus.

A God whose opening line is "Do not be afraid," is not a scary God.

Everybody's a Critic

Rodney Wallace Kennedy

Jesus offers cultural critique: "But to what will I compare this generation?" Let me count the ways. Culture critique is a growth industry in America. From scholarly tomes to barbershop chatter, everybody knows exactly what is wrong with America. I hope you had a wonderful fourth of July and that you really took some time to remember how fortunate we are and what a marvelous place this is to live, but it seems everybody's a critic. We have created a society of mistrust, suspicion, and deep criticism. The lines are drawn and people mostly now congregate with others of like minds and like politics and like ways and they avoid the other—the nasty, threatening other. America is becoming homogenized into scared little communities in the midst of diversity.

Jesus is not like the cultural despisers of our time. This is not Rush Limbaugh pontificating prejudice or Rachel Maddow waving the flag of liberalism. This is not the brilliant satire of Jon Stewart or the angry protestations of Ann Coulter. In any event, this is not a commentator popping off; this is Jesus: the second person of the Trinity; the Son of God, the one crucified, buried, dead, and raised. This is Jesus the way, the truth, and the life.

There is an important distinction to make at the outset: critical thinking is not the same as criticism. Michael Roth, president of Wesleyan University says:

> A common way to show that one has sharpened one's critical thinking is to display an ability to see through or undermine statements made by (or beliefs held by) others. Thus, our best students are really good at one aspect of critical thinking—being critical. For many students today, being smart means being critical. But

this participation, being entirely negative, is not only seriously unsatisfying; it is ultimately counterproductive.[1]

We have become too good at showing why any proposed solution will not work, too obsessed with debunking others. And this criticism spills over into our everyday judgments about everything and everybody. Go to any church and listen closely and you will hear the murmuring, the relentless criticism aimed at the worship, the music, the sermons, the people. Jesus calls us to be Christian; we have become critics. Christians busy themselves with social criticism and are in constant uproar about the behavior of people they don't even know. We criticize people we don't know for believing stuff we don't understand.

Opinion rules, especially opinion that begins with "I don't like it." What about the Apostle's Creed? "I don't like it." What about contemporary music? "I don't like it." We have created an entire class of self-satisfied debunkers. "That won't work." "I don't like that."

Leaders swim in an ocean of criticism. Anyone with a new idea attracts the sharks. Research shows that criticism is a leading cause of ministers leaving the church. About 1,500 pastors leave the ministry every month. Try to govern anything from a village to a nation and the critics howl. Try to coach little league soccer or the USA World Cup soccer team and the critics know more than the coaches. The bigger the challenge you take on, the more criticism you are going to face.

Church is not meant to be a house of criticism but a house of compassion. Yet we are more often debunkers than disciples.

Criticism is not all it's cracked up to be. Criticism exacts a huge emotional price. It wears out the critic. Like an emotional boomerang, the criticism comes back to bite the critic with an exhaustion that is mind numbing. Exhaustion comes from always being upset about something or somebody. Aren't you weary of hearing how awful fellow Americans, fellow Christians are? Jesus offers to take away our weariness because he knows that our foray each day as childish participants in the marketplace of critics is exhausting us.

---

1. Michael Roth, "Young Minds in Critical Condition," *The New York Times*, May 10, 2014.

What's a Southern Boy Doing in Dayton, Ohio?

Rodney Wallace Kennedy

Sure, the Civil War ended in 1865, but for those of us lucky enough to be born in the South, having endured our "fall," we have resources forged in suffering, shame, and defeat not known to others. Yet even with all those gifts and the advantage of the Southern con—the ability to make your enemies think you are stupid—there is a nervousness that hits you when you cross the Mason Dixon line into enemy territory. I felt it as I faced the congregation of First Baptist Church Dayton on the Sunday of my "call" sermon.

One should never be nervous about the "call" sermon. After all, any preacher should have at least one good sermon. The congregation is mostly going to go with the recommendation of the pastoral search committee, which is the reason I was standing in the pulpit in the first place. Still, there's tension. Some folks hear a Southern accent and instead of magnolia blossoms, boiled shrimp, and honeysuckle, they have visions of undereducated rednecks, fried bacon drippings, boiled crawfish, and biscuits. This of course brings into question not only Yankee prejudice but a complete lack of culinary sophistication.

In the introduction of my "call" sermon, I felt it best to get everything on the table so I told the congregation that I embraced Will Campbell's definition of Christianity: "We are all bastards and God loves us anyway."[1] Well, they thought I said, "We are all Baptists and God loves us anyway." The Southern accent, right? On reflection, if they thought I said "Baptists" they should have been even more offended than they would have been by the word "bastard." In any event, no permanent damage was done.

---

1. Campbell, reflecting on the death of Jonathan Daniel in Connelly, *Will Campbell and the Soul of the South*, 100.

After worship, there was a congregational meeting—a question and answer free-for-all. Church members were allowed to ask me questions and all the questions had a common theme. I was from the South and therefore they were worried that I would be too conservative. Somehow I survived this inquisition and the vote to call me as the next pastor was 114–4. Six months later the congregation worried I was too liberal.

Liberal or conservative, Baptists are a resilient people. First Baptist Church had been founded by a group of stalwart Calvinists—a group with deep convictions but a sweeter spirit than the current bunch of hyper-Calvinists holding some Southern Baptist seminaries and churches hostage. In any event, when Alexander Campbell swept through Dayton, the pastor and the entire congregation was swept away by the spirit of revivalism. Only eight members voted to "keep the stand." Those eight Calvinists are named on a plaque in our narthex and they are recalled each year on Founder's Sunday. In 1912, J. C. Massee became the senior pastor. As historian William Trollinger notes in an essay on the history of First Baptist Church Dayton, "Massee was strongly committed to Biblical inerrancy and dispensational premillennialism. Given his prominence it was not surprising that he was present for the first meeting of the World's Christian Fundamentals Association in Philadelphia in May 1919. Not coincidentally, in 1919 Massee also left First Baptist of Dayton for the more prominent pulpit of Tremont Temple in Boston; from this location he served as one of the major leaders of the emergent fundamentalist movement (although, in keeping with the Calvinists who founded First Baptist, he ended up being excoriated by fundamentalist leaders for not being sufficiently fundamentalist)."[2] Those early Calvinists and Dr. Massee saved First Baptist Church for a Catholic-Baptist, post-liberal, full-orbed Arminian who also happens to be a Southerner. I rejoice at the strength of the First Baptist Church and even more that I am privileged to be the lead pastor for now these thirteen years. There can be no higher privilege.

2. Trollinger, "The History of the First Baptist Church."

I Am a Redneck

Rodney Wallace Kennedy

I am a redneck. Jeff Foxworthy became famous by saying, "You might be a redneck if . . . ." Well, in my case there is no "if." I am a redneck. Sure, I put hunks of yellow meal cornbread into tall, cold glasses of milk. I have milked cows and been thrown from the back of a stubborn Shetland pony (try living that down in the country). Purple-hull peas and speckled butterbeans are still my favorite vegetables. Good luck trying to find either of those delicacies in the unwashed Midwest where rutabagas and Brussels sprouts grow like kudzu and the kudzu would probably taste better if you added a slab of bacon to the pot. Almost everyone makes fun of rednecks. Hell, we make fun of ourselves, but we are not as stupid as you may have been led to believe. People talking slow are not always slow.

Especially outside of the South, people are concerned about rednecks. As soon as I greet someone new here in the great Midwest, the response is instant: "You must not be from here." I ask, "What gave it away?" "The accent," people will say. I have discovered that there are advantages at this point. It is always helpful in a debate about postmodern philosophy to let your opponent feel you are inferior, not quite up to snuff. People often get sloppy when they think you are not smart. We call it the "Southern con" and we are really good at using it on other people.

But I digress. I want you to know that I'm a redneck. Growing up in NipNTuck, Louisiana (and yes, that is a real town and it had to do with how tough it was to make a living out of rock-hard soil), we went to church on Sunday morning, Sunday night, and Wednesday. We went to two weeks of revival every year. There was homecoming, dinner-on-the-ground, and all day singing. The food was redneck from the smothered steak with gravy and rice to the fried cornbread to the fresh garden tomatoes, potato salad, speckled butterbeans, and purple hull peas. I am a redneck!

Baseball was considered God's favorite sport. While we were not allowed to go hunting or fishing on Sunday, we were allowed to play baseball at the church baseball park. Obviously God approved of baseball since it was the only sanctioned Sunday afternoon activity. We played baseball on Monday, Tuesday, Thursday, Friday, Saturday, and Sunday; the rest of the time we were in church.

I memorized enough Scripture to last a lifetime. Memory Bible drill and Intermediate Bible Sword Drill filled our Sunday night Training Union. To this day, I am quite at home in a Bible verse slinging contest. Truth be told, I loved memorizing Bible verses and winning the contests. When I quote Scripture in a sermon, the King James Bible version comes out of my mouth instead of the New Revised Standard Version. I memorized the King James and it went really deep and has stayed for the duration.

When a passel of redneck preachers and deacons ordained me to the gospel ministry in 1967, they laid hands on me, gave me a Scofield Reference Bible and told me to go preach that book and I have been doing that ever since. It is a dangerous thing to give a Redneck a Bible and a PhD and tell him he can say whatever he pleases.

On every hill in our community, there was a brother or a sister of my dad. I have fifty-seven first cousins. We looked after one another. On a summer day, you had lunch at whichever aunt's house you happened to be playing. If you bothered one Kennedy, you had to deal with the whole bunch. We go way back and we are permanently stained by the red clay dirt in those north Louisiana hills. My granddaddy made moonshine whiskey and once had a knock-down fight on Main Street with the sheriff. Somehow the sheriff had forgotten to pay for the previous week's moonshine delivery. Grandpa won that fight when he bit off the sheriff's ear. I am a redneck!

Church, family, more church, baseball, Jesus, and all that food! Smile when you call me a redneck and know that when it comes to argument, that fine practice of Aristotle's rhetoric, I will do my damnest to give you my best shot, funny accent and all. But I do wonder why people from Minnesota and Maine think that Southerners talk funny! God bless y'all.

Why It Is Christian to Oppose Government-Sponsored Worship in Public Schools

Rodney Wallace Kennedy

Some Christians want the public schools to do their work for them. There's all this angst about prayer being removed from public schools. It's not true. The purveyors of this propaganda surely know this isn't a real issue. It is a made for the cultural wars issue and its purpose is money and votes not prayers by children. Seriously, what's going on with Christians agitating for government-sponsored worship in public schools? I can't bring myself to give support to compulsory, generic prayer separated from its mother— worship. This doesn't mean I am opposed to students praying. I'm sure students and teachers pray at school.

While I am amused by the irony of Christian literalists campaigning for a symbolic act of prayer in schools, I am not surprised. The question of prayer in public schools is too prized by preacher-politicians to give it up. In the past ten years I have heard preachers blame everything from the breakdown of the family to the frequency of hurricanes to the lack of prayer in public schools. David Barton, the amateur Texas historian, has repeated his story that SAT scores started falling after the Supreme Court ruling on public prayer so often that he actually believes it. I'm not buying it. Barton wrote a book allegedly about the lies of Thomas Jefferson. The publisher took the almost unheard action of removing the book from all bookstores because the lies turned out to be those of Mr. Barton.

Historian David Krause has chronicled the rise of the public religion that harps so much on prayers in public schools. The actual goal was to promote capitalism more than Christian faith. He demonstrates how President Eisenhower's administration "succeeded in sacralizing the state, swiftly implementing a host of religious ceremonies and symbols and thereby inscribing—quite literally, in many ways—an apparently permanent public religion on the institution of American government."[1] The irony is that Eisenhower didn't possess any actual Christian convictions beyond that of a Christian America. He reluctantly agrees to become a member of First Presbyterian Church in Washington, and he sought to downplay it at all costs. "He had agreed to join only after Revered Edward L. R. Elson promised to be discreet. But as Eisenhower wrote angrily in his diary, 'we were scarcely home before the fact [of his baptism] was being publicized, by the pastor, to the hilt. The president screamed to his press secretary, Jim Hagerty, 'You go and tell that goddam minister that if he gives out one more story about my religious faith I won't join his goddam church!'"[2]

All the arguments for and against government-sponsored prayer, worship, and Bible courses have been falling like rain for the proverbial "forty days and nights." There are some practical concerns that still need to be offered. Beyond the incessant arguments, imagine the actual practice of government prayer. What would a government-produced prayer sound like in a public school in America? I can imagine the student reading the prayer that some government agent in the interfaith department of multifaith relationships sent. "Our father, mother, guru, great spirit, divine one, good guy, man in the sky, give us this day our daily white, black, Russian, Italian, Hungarian, focaccia, marble rye bread."

Now, imagine the teacher given the responsibility to teach a course in the Bible. There will be a world of difference between a fundamentalist Christian with a propensity for "literalistic" interpretation and a liberal Christian trained in the historical criticism of the Bible. A new fight would break out over the curriculum and the teachers qualified to teach the course. How would the school board ever find an objective, non-biased teacher for the Bible course? Almost no one lacks opinions about the Bible, even people that have never read the Bible. There's something about the Bible that resists attempts at sanitizing its contents and making it bland discussions about biblical history. One can only go so far talking about what happened to the Jebusites before encountering the living God.

The suggestion that the Bible be taught as literature or as history fails to do justice to a book that is about God and therefore requires theology. Theology then requires study of issues that go far beyond literature. The Christians would never be able to agree on the theologians that would teach

1. Krause, *One Nation Under God*, Kindle ed., loc. 1762.
2. Ibid, loc. 1486.

the Bible course. Would the school hire a professor from Cedarville University or from Candler School of Theology?

Perhaps the overriding practical concern is the students that Christians presume are panting to sign up for courses about the Bible. The push for Christian intrusion into public schools assumes that students actually want to pray and study the Bible. School districts in Texas and other states have recently dropped Bible courses from the curriculum because not enough students register for the courses. In contrast, I offer a piece of anecdotal evidence. Oakwood High School, in Dayton, Ohio offers a high school class in religions of the world. There are three sections offered each year and the classes are always full. The students are energized, interested, and bright. The class offers students an amazing introduction into the study of religion and the varying practices of religion around the world. The course is offered under the auspices of the English department. The purpose of the course is education not evangelism.

I suggest that Christians as a sign of hospitality and humility give up the attempt to have government and public school teachers to do their work for them. Put down the Bible and step away from the public school and take the gospel into the streets, the highways, and the byways, and trust the gospel to do its work there as before. In exercises of hospitality and goodness, offer the Muslims the place of priority in praying at school at designated times for religious expression and offer Christian students a space for Bible study without school employees teaching. Will Campbell suggested that we can all kneel on a prayer rug, put our heads to the ground, and pray. While praying, we could promise that we will stop killing one another in the name of God. I'm sure our Muslim brothers have extra prayer clothes.

I don't want the school doing my church work for me. As a Christian who believes in "family values," I want public schools to welcome all children and leave decisions about religion, worship, and prayer to families, synagogues, mosques, churches, and other religious institutions. "Let us pray" belongs in worship not between science and math classes.

Christians, in particular, should remember that Jesus warns people not to turn prayer into a theatrical production. "All these people making a regular show out of their prayers, hoping for stardom! Do you think God sits in a box seat?" (Matt 6:5, *The Message*). "But thou, when thou prayest, enter into thy closet, and when thou hast shut thy door, pray to thy Father which seeth in secret" (Matt 6:6, *The King James Version*).

Children attend public schools from every nation and culture in our world. Public schools are the gathering place where children are required to do the tough work of integration, assimilation, and understanding that adults rarely are willing to tackle. Isn't it part of our national shame that we always send children to do the hard work of breaking down barriers? I still have vivid memories of the children walking past all those angry people on the first day of integration in Little Rock, Arkansas. We send children to do the dirty work while we hide in segregated and gated communities.

A pox on government-composed prayers in school. I remain hopeful that Christians will awaken to the greater needs of clothing, feeding, and educating the thousands of poor children that populate our public schools every day. It will take more than the prayers of political opportunists to bring those worthy goals of justice to pass.

McKnight's Dry Goods Store

Rodney Wallace Kennedy

McKnight's Dry Goods Store, on Main Street, Clinton, Louisiana was church for me, Monday through Saturday, for four wonderful years. The service began each morning at 7:30 a.m. The elements for the daily sacrament of Holy Communion was Community dark roast coffee and homemade tea cakes. The high priest of our church was "Big" Ikey McKnight. He had previously been a deacon in the First Baptist Church but no longer attended since a new pastor, filled with the awful theology of hyper-Calvinism, had cleaned the rolls of all who wouldn't abide by his pastoral authority, invalidated the church constitution, and shut down all church boards and committees. So now Ikey went to church in the back of his own store.

And what a store it was. There was a counter in the back of the store and chairs for people to sit. The church was small and most days there were about seven of us in attendance. We were Baptists and Methodists and agnostics; Republicans and Democrats, and LSU Tiger fans. All opinions were allowed space in the morning conversation but not all opinions were treated with respect. Within minutes of the first sip of coffee, the conversation would fire up on all cylinders. The Rev. McKnight would throw a hot topic on the table and sit back and listen to us all raise hell. Salty language, raised voices, hostile jabs—you would thought you had dropped in a on a Baptist church business meeting where they were attempting to fire the pastor.

Once in a while, a stranger would stumble into the meeting. A newly ordained Presbyterian Church in America pastor dropped in one Monday morning. He had no idea that we were a nest of Arminians with enough free will theology to share with the world. With undaunted courage he held out against the crowd, and while no one ever bought his austere theology, he won our grudging respect because he kept showing up every morning and throwing his hat into the ring. Nice young man with a tough job trying to start a church in the land of the over-churched.

I never knew that McKnight's was church for me until I moved to the big city. I miss McKnight's Church of Assorted and Sordid Conversations. I miss it more than I can say.

I miss the conversations about politics, baseball, football, current events, gossip, philosophy, and theology. Church met every day. We gathered in the back of the story at 7:30 a.m., six days a week, people of various convictions and plenty of piss and vinegar. We fought like dogs and cats over politics and religion. People got mad, went home swearing never to return. Next morning they were back, coffee cup in one hand, tea cakes in the other, and mouth running at full speed. They had already forgotten the verbal beating they had endured the previous morning.

I miss it for a lot of reasons but mostly because I have not been able to find another group willing to have those kinds of conversations. Today we are afraid to talk to one another across party lines. There is a huge gulf fixed between us and we are the less for it.

If two or three people were willing to risk it, I'd be glad to provide the coffee and the tea cakes. Daily communion that fills the mind, the heart, and the soul—absolutely heavenly!

There's No Business Like Church Business

Rodney Wallace Kennedy

There's no business like church business. A lay leader in the congregation called and asked me to take a ride in the country with him on a Saturday morning. He picked me up early that morning and we took a leisurely ride in the country. The magnolias were in full bloom and the honeysuckle was wrapping its parasitic vines in terrifying beauty all along the country road. Silence for the first fifteen minutes filled the long sleek Cadillac.

Finally, the lay leader blurted out, "Preacher you have the budget of our little church too high."

Startled by the concept, I asked him if we were behind in our budget giving. "No," he replied, "but that's not the point. Our budget has never been this high in history and it's just making me uneasy."

I reassured him as best I could that the people would continue their faithful giving and that the church would benefit from the increased opportunities for mission. He was not reassured. So the ride ended in an uneasy truce.

Some months later I asked the executive council to consider building a new parsonage. The old parsonage grew mold along the walls at a pace faster than scrubbing the walls could foil. The roof leaked. You didn't need a television weather report in the morning because if the wind was blowing from the north, it blew right through the cracks in the wall. The furniture would have embarrassed the folks at Good Will. The parsonage should have been replaced thirty years earlier.

The extended debate about a new parsonage elicited reasons to oppose that smothered the reasons for building like sausage gravy on a hot biscuit. The lay leader from the Saturday morning country ride chimed in, "I told preacher that the budget was too high for our little church and that it would come to no good. So now we know that he has been conniving to get a new parsonage all along. I make a motion that we reject this political move." A quick second and a quicker vote killed all hopes of a new parsonage.

A year later a family offered to donate an acre of land next door to the church for a new parsonage. Nine signatures were required to complete the transaction. Four members of the family lived out of town. One family member held out—a doctor from Chicago. Finally, I talked to his wife and I'm not going to tell you how I managed to make the deal, but she got her husband to sign the deed, and the church had an acre of ground. Also, I found a contractor who agreed to build the new parsonage at cost. All the church needed to do was provide the materials. This was surely too good a deal to reject. At the next meeting of the Trustees, the contractor made a presentation and offered to build the house for the church. No one said anything about the deal costing too much. The decision this time was cut and dried around the flat denial that a new parsonage would be needed. It was a luxury they could do without. Again a quick motion and second and a resounding defeat.

After another year I moved to a new church. The first month of the new pastor's tenure, the church voted to build a new parsonage at twice the price I had originally offered. For my part, I was grateful the new pastor and his wife would no longer have to fight the mold on the walls. As for the fear of change that hovered over the church "like fog on a coffin lid" (Allan Gurganus), there wasn't a thing that could be done.

In the politics of congregations, a politics that no seminary can possibly prepare pastors to face, a new parsonage was cause enough for gratitude! There's no business like church business!

Made a Preacher at Twelve

Rodney Wallace Kennedy

At the age of twelve, the good, God-fearing people of Antioch Baptist Church of NipNTuck, Louisiana, made me a preacher. That was fifty years ago and the idea still haunts me. John Claypool, hearing my story, said it was a miracle I wasn't in a mental institution. Well, I have been institutionalized my entire life by church and academy.

My wife suggested that I needed to tell someone about it. In her mind, it will make me feel better. I'm not convinced, because I have often found that good Baptists are not interested in honest preachers. But since it is unlikely that good, God-fearing, afraid of the "light" born again Christians will dare to read this, I'm telling you. As to whether or not it makes me feel any better, we will have to wait and see.

When I was twelve, seventy-seven serious believers raised their hands to say, "Give the boy a license to preach. He's weak, sickly, won't ever be able to get a real job. Let him preach." At least a dozen loud "Amens" filled the white clapboard church and that settled it. I was now a preacher. The year was 1962.

That's right. A preacher. A twelve-year-old kid who loved baseball and squirrel hunting was now carrying a license to preach. Sure, I memorized Bible verses for the Bible Memory Drill competition. The key word —"competition." Sure, I'd been praying in "big church" since I was eight. But being precocious and having above average reading skills are not strong enough reasons to make a kid a preacher. No group of people should ever be allowed to give a twelve-year-old kid a license to preach. I was still three years from being old enough to drive, five years from being drafted by the Army to die in the rice paddies of Vietnam, and eight years from being old enough to vote and drink whiskey. But at the age of twelve, I was made a preacher. I was interested in curves, throwing a sharp-breaking one in baseball games and watching girls walk down Main Street on a sultry July summer in yellow-polka dot sun backs. But out of the blue, I was thrown the curve that settled my life like Quick-Crete. I should have scrawled my name in the concrete and written "Help," but I was too dumb not to be excited. After all, I was the only twelve-year-old preacher for as far as my known world then extended.

In all fairness, this was not the preposterous event I have made it out to be. The protest comes from "looking back" on the experience as an adult and wondering how I survived. Being called to preach at a young age was not considered unusual in my "neck of the woods." After all, I had been "saved" and baptized at the age of eight. The language of the Bible surrounded our home life. We were, after all, a pious and deeply committed people. The publication *The Sword of the Lord* came to our home and we read every word. The imprint of Landmark Baptists and "born again" theology and the sense that God was actually still talking out loud to people pervaded our atmosphere. The only people ever shocked by this story are people from Ohio or New York or Minnesota. Catholics don't get it. Episcopalians can't grasp it. But in the hill country, among the Baptists, being called to preach at a young age was as natural as drinking from a cold-water spring. After all, Samuel was young when the call came to him. And Jeremiah. And Jesus was twelve when he astounded the religious leaders in the church.

Well, not everybody was giddy about my prospects as a preacher. As my non-church going, Church of Christ bred granddaddy put it, I'd become "a god-damn freak show. The boy might as well run off and join Barnum and Bailey." This turns out to have been a prophetic pronouncement by the decidedly non-prophetic whiskey-making patriarch of our family.

For four years, my daddy drove me around the country on Sunday morning to preach in out-of-the-way little Baptist churches. One church had a roof with green shingles on one side and blue on the other, a sure sign that the business meeting had been a fight over the color of the shingles and nobody won. Another church had men sitting on one side and women on the other side. Daddy always brought along a box, made of solid oak, to place behind the pulpit. I would stand on the box in order to see over the pulpit and preach to the expectant congregation, people hanging on every word of the twelve-year-old, evidence of God's presence, preaching wonder.

Also in the year of being twelve, I made the Little League All-Star team. The night of the All-Star game, Daddy had to work overtime at the

Commercial Solvents Chemical Corporation. That means he missed the happiest night of my life up to that point. Three innings of perfect pitching with seven strikeouts and a three-for-three night at the plate with a home run and two doubles made me that happy. Daddy worked all night and then worked his regular shift the next day. I was standing in the yard playing catch with my sister when Daddy came home. Even though he was coming home from a thirty-two-hour shift at the plant, he bounded across the yard. Yelling "that's my boy. That's my boy," he grabbed me up into his arms and swung me around. Word about my big night as an All-Star had made it to the plant that morning when the other dads came to work. It is not exactly, "You are my beloved Son with whom I am well-pleased," but it was close enough to mark me for life as a son who was loved and a daddy who was proud. My dad—giver of the gifts of baseball and religion!

My idols were the roaring evangelists who rolled through our red-clay, pine-littered community twice every year—once in the spring and again in August—to preach rip-roaring sermons about heaven and hell, against Darwin and liberals, for eternal salvation and being born again. I not only loved the excitement generated by this hot-wired preaching, I wanted to be those preachers. They would thunder against drinking and college-educated, seminary-trained preachers. "That seminary will ruin a young man" was the constant refrain. My own sixth-grade dropout dad told me, "Those preachers never finished college and they are just mad about it. Ignore them because you are getting an education."

Whether or not the seminary education "ruined" me depends on the person or persons you ask. I am grateful for those preachers because they put in me a burning desire to preach with passion. While I have moved far from the theological assertions of my childhood, my love of Scripture and my passion for preaching have remained steadfast.

After fifty-two years I have only one definitive thought: "Thank you Jesus, thank you for making me a preacher!" I wouldn't have wanted it any other way. Those good Christians were right. Preaching was my calling and so it remains to this day. Stepping into the pulpit on Sunday morning in the magnificent Gothic cathedral that is the First Baptist Church of Dayton, Ohio, I look around at the stained glass ceiling, the eloquent arches, the pipes of the organ reaching for the sky, and the people gathered in the name of Jesus who has promised to be present, and I take a deep breath and say, "Thank you Jesus, for making me a preacher!"

The Parsonage:
Where You Can't Make this Stuff Up!

Rodney Wallace Kennedy

For six years, I lived in the parsonage next door to the church. The two-story white-shingled church stood alongside Highway 1 South between Alexandria, Louisiana and Echo, Louisiana. The other three sides contained a soybean field. There was nothing for eight miles in either direction from the church. Standing there like a lighthouse on a Gulf of Mexico inlet or a sentinel at his post, the church alone would have attracted visitors. But outside the church, up against the highway stood a twenty-five foot neon sign. Every bug, mosquito, and stray human found its way to the shining light in the night.

Almost everything of importance happened at night. In the full light of day the parsonage was an ordinary, three-bedroom, two-bath, single-story dwelling—ordinary, plain, a house like a million others. After midnight it was the stuff of mystery and intrigue running the gamut of human experience. Part gas station, part repair shop, part counseling center, part bed and breakfast, that house was like falling down Alice's rabbit hole or walking through a door and entering a strange world of troubled, confused, and needy human beings.

Deacon dropped by one night and said, "Preacher, I plant purple hull peas in between the soybean plants in my field. The soybean plants provide shade and the peas produce twice as much as usual. Drop by the field in the morning and pick all the peas you want." Thinking the deacon was a man of his word, I showed up early and picked twelve bushels of peas. "Damn, preacher, I had no idea you'd pick that many of my peas." Well, the way I figure, a deal is a deal and he never asked or I would have told him that I was a pea picker since I was knee high to a duck's back in NipNTuck. He never offered me any more peas, but after shelling, blanching, and bagging those twelve bushels, I had enough peas for two winters.

No one ever bothered to tell me that all the deacons and Sunday school teachers—that's about twenty people—had keys to the back door of the parsonage. The second Sunday of my time as pastor, I walked into the kitchen at 7:00 a.m. to make coffee and I wasn't wearing anything more than God clothed me in when I entered this cosmos screaming and kicking. There were two deacons and a woman sitting at the breakfast table reading the Sunday newspaper and having a conversation about the previous night's LSU football game. I'm not sure if the scream from the lady came first or me busting down the door between the kitchen and the dining room. I got the hell out of there. No one ever spoke of this moment and I had the lock changed. No one ever asked me about it.

Deacons told me they only paid $25 per month on the utility bill. Asked why, the chairman said, "I would drive by at night and all the lights would be on in every room of the parsonage so we stopped paying for the electricity bill." Well, that pastor had four children and a wife, and they needed the lights on in every room. In any event, we worked out a deal and I kept the lights out, especially in the bedroom.

One day, a lady tried to beat the train but didn't make it. It took the train 300 yards to stop right in front of the parsonage. I ran across the highway and to the tracks. The lady's head was lying on the steering wheel, a hole the size of a silver-dollar in her forehead. No doubt she was dead. On the floorboard of the front passenger seat, with the ripped metal of the car wrapped around it like a cocoon, was a five-year-old girl. She didn't have a scratch on her.

People riding the rails would stop at the parsonage for food. We kept a supply of white bread and Spam on the back porch to provide food.

Knock on the back door, and there was a church member offering a sack of fresh tomatoes, purple hull peas, speckled butter beans, watermelon, fresh corn, okra, and cucumbers. I once made the mistake of saying I didn't like cucumbers and folks started bringing me cucumbers fixed in every possible way. I learned not to tell people about my culinary dislikes or my true feelings about cats.

I once tried to build a fence between the church and the parsonage for some privacy, but with no experience in fence building, I stretched the wire using my Volkswagen Bug, and managed only to pull down the entire project. People sitting over in the church yard laughed until they cried but no one lifted a finger to help. They didn't want a fence between their parsonage and their church.

You would think it would be a perfect set-up. Walk across the driveway every morning, a mere twenty-five steps, and I was in the church and at work. *Perfect* is never one of the words that jumps to the front of the line when I think of living in that parsonage. Yet I miss it. I miss the adventure that came from the knock on the door, especially the front door. That meant it was a stranger in need of some Christian hospitality. I felt needed, useful. I felt as if I was the ranger responsible for that eight-mile stretch of lonely Highway 1.

Now, there are no knocks on the door as I live on the sixteenth floor of a downtown condo and no one brings fresh vegetables. No one shows up with trouble that requires action on my part. I miss the creative stories, the mile-high lies that people poured into my naïve mind.

It never crossed my mind to be irritated or upset. Somehow the notion that I was guarding an eight-mile stretch of Highway 1 South had been velcroed into my mind. At the knock on the door, I would spring into action. It's a wonder I didn't wear Superman pajamas to bed with a cape. What joy to be useful in a way that had finality to it.

A medium-size white man stood at the door of the parsonage with a chain saw in his left hand and standing with a 10-year-old boy at his right hand. It was about two in the morning and I couldn't take my eyes off the chain saw. "Sorry, Reverend, I know this looks peculiar. I don't mean you any harm, but I need some help." Convinced that this wasn't going to be a chain saw massacre, I invited the man and his son to come inside out of the frigid 15 degree weather (that's really cold for the northern edge of southern Louisiana). "Would y'all like some coffee and hot chocolate?" I hurried to start the coffee and heat the milk for instant cocoa, but the chain saw filled my imagination. I couldn't wait to hear this story.

"What brings you out in this cold so late in the night?"

"My wife chased us out of the house." I wanted to ask if she had a shotgun because I couldn't believe that a chain saw-armed man would have budged from a warm house even when it contained an angry woman, but I waited for the story. A story will just flat die if you get too nosy and ask too many damn questions. "We had a fight and I just can't stand all that yelling and cussing, so I grabbed my chain saw and the boy, and high-tailed out of there."

"What's your name?"

"Larry Taylor. My family owns a bunch of service stations around Alexandria."

"And your son?"

"Larry, Jr."

"Why the chain saw?"

"It was sitting there by the door and so I grabbed it on the way out."

My goodness, I thought. This was definitely under the category of "you can't make this stuff up," but I couldn't imagine anyone of a sound mind believing me when I told this story.

"How come you couldn't just stay home and work out your problem?"

"She's just meaner than a cotton-mouth water moccasin when she's mad. Most of the time, she's sweet and easy-going but when her eyes cross and she gets something stuck in her craw, all hell breaks loose. She starts chewing on some little tiny insult or hint of disrespect over the first cup of morning coffee and by three in the afternoon she's a regular spitfire. She gnaws on the minor little something until it grows into a hideous monster and then takes it out on everyone in the house. Only thing left for a man to do is run. There's no way you can stand there and take that kind of unmitigated wrath. She uses words like a straight-edge razor and skins you alive with it."

Making a mental note, "I hope to God I never encounter this cold, hard case of a woman," I asked, "Well, how can I help you?"

"We need a ride to Marksville." This was a small town about twenty miles south of the parsonage. The sheriff of the parish was once reelected while serving a jail sentence for malfeasance in office. I swear to God, that's the truth. Look, a man with a chain saw, who was afraid of his wife, deserved a twenty-minute ride if it brought him peace of mind. So we finished off the coffee, piled into my Chevy Impala and made the short drive to Marksville.

The man didn't seem to really know where in Marksville he wanted to go, but finally pointed out a bar and asked me to let them out there. Trying not to be judgmental, I assumed his sister or some blood relative owned the bar, and he was going there to tell his family about his predicament and get a place to spend the night until his wife calmed down a bit. He kept looking over his shoulder as if expecting her to show up with guns blazing at any moment.

Driving back to the parsonage at around three in the morning, I went down to my house justified. I had saved a man from certain death, a man afraid to face his wife even with a chain saw in his hands. As religious folks like to say, "It was a mystery to me." Yet life at the parsonage was as incarnational as ministry ever gets. I was now prepared for the humanity of church that thankfully always exceeds the syrupy piety that masquerades as Christianity.

Evolution as Faith Partner

Rodney Wallace Kennedy

Preachers are steamed over evolution. Call it the E word as in a bigger curse word than the F bomb. To hear them preach, the E word is the anti-Christ, the beast out of the sea, the assembled masses of Satan's legions, the great dragon. Evolution gets blamed for everything except the common cold. Some of these preachers are so obsessed with creation doctrine they have truncated the Bible to the literalistic reading of only the book of Genesis. And even Genesis has two creation stories. Isn't that just like God to keep us guessing?

But now we don't have to guess because we don't have to choose between the Bible and science. Faced with the dastardly dualism of the creationist, like Carlyle Marney as an eight-year-old listening to the adults go on about Darrow the dragon in the Scopes Trial, you secretly start pulling for the dragon. Evolution is not a dragon; it is established science.

Yet millions of Americans and their preachers consider evolution the deadly enemy. In its place they have a theory: creationism and its badly dressed cousin Intelligent Design. There are two basic flaws with scientific creationism: bad science and bad religion. Ken Ham's ministry is called Answers in Genesis (AIG). Well, the answers are in the gospel. The answers about God, creation, salvation, and life are in Jesus Christ.

Being silent about creationism is not an option. These Christians are so obsessed with the beginning of the earth they have little concern for how quickly we could all be turned to nuclear ash. So you want me to be silent about the most controversial subject in America today and allow the creationists to go on and on with their unbiblical, untrue, dangerous ideology? I apologize in advance to you but I can't do that.

Why do so many Americans reject evolution? Kenneth Miller, Brown University biology professor: "The truth is that evolution strikes at the heart of what and who we are. Did we arise in a flash of divine inspiration or did we crawl slowly out of the muck? Christians often answer these questions the wrong way."[1] Opponents of evolution believe that evolution teaches us that we are accidents, nothing more than Darwin's beasts, that we are not special. Evolution actually teaches the opposite of these false charges. We are not mistakes of nature.

Science searches for truth with unrelenting mental fury. If a theory is false, science will uncover it, reject it, and throw it on the pile. A science professor had a sign posted in his lab: "Nothing is more terrible than the murder of a beautiful theory by a gang of ugly facts." Among many Christians, beautiful theories are all that matter. When you discover that something you believe is false, no matter how emotionally satisfying the belief has been, you should drop it rather than double down and dig in your heels and continue to insist that the belief is true. In the final analysis, good science wins and bad science fails. And good science wins on the basis of the evidence. Science keeps doing science, searching for truth, wrestling with the evidence; creationism keeps denying science, doing no research, and saying, "We disagree with these experts." When it comes to argument, you have to do better than that. Bad religion keeps repeating failed theology of the past.

Science, at home in university classrooms and research labs, now has to fight for its life in courtrooms crowded with preachers and local school boards. What in the world are scientists doing in a courtroom? I can barely take political advice from politicians; I certainly don't want them running our science labs. Quite simply: teach religion in Sunday school; teach science in public schools.

Science has been good to us. Why would we want to believe it to be satanic? With little effort, you could make a list of the ways science has improved life and made life easier, more enjoyable, safer, healthier, and increased the possibility that we will live to be 100 years old. Medicine is science—evolutionary science. Without science, some of us would have died decades ago.

Here's a different perspective for Christians. Accept the biological evidence: the earth is billions of years old. Life appeared gradually, step by step guided by God, and according to Proverbs, wisdom was God's constant

1. Miller, *Only a Theory*, 135.

companion over hundreds of millions of years. Wisdom cries out, "The Lord created me at the beginning of his work, the first of his acts of long ago. Ages ago I was set up, at the first, before the beginning of the earth."

Our family tree has been a long time in development, from a seed a mighty tree; from a cell to a universe larger than our imagination. Just as Scripture claims we are made from the dust of the universe itself—star dust! We require a cosmos of inconceivable age, finely tuned fundamental constants to stoke the fires of trillions of suns, and a balance of light and heavy elements forged in the embers of dying stars. These ingredients make up a "recipe" for our universe, a step-by-step guide to creating life from the very forces that shape galaxies and fill the earth with light and color. Where did this come from? It all came from God. It is, as physicist Freeman Dyson, puts it, a "universe that knew we were coming." We occupy a special place in the universe and that place is, in the words of St. James, "that we should be a kind of first fruits of [God's] creatures."

The church has more important work to do than opposing science. Our work is the praise of creation. The Bible doesn't have a theology of creation—a creationism. The Bible has a doxology of creation. Genesis is a poem, a hymn of praise with a refrain: It was good! Job 37–40 is a veritable doxology to creation, and it was written centuries before Genesis 1. The questions of God to Job should be posed to all creationists:

> Where were you when I laid the foundation of the earth? Tell me, if you have understanding. Where were you when the morning stars sang together and all the heavenly beings shouted for joy? Have you commanded the morning since your days began, and caused the dawn to know its place. Declare, if you know all this. Surely you know, for you were born then, and the number of your days is great! (Job 37:4–7, 21).

Confidence, joy, and patience: These three are given to us. "These are the gifts of God for the people of God." I would say that is not a bad Sunday of work. To God be the glory!

A Meal

Rodney Wallace Kennedy

Walking on eggshells, tiptoeing through tulips, living in Never Land—these are our responses to race. Year after year, we keep showing up at our own churches because integration remains an elusive dream. Even in our public schools, there's all this chatter that integration has not worked and it is time to go back to community schools or charter schools or home schooling. The issue of race, what Will Campbell always insisted was a theological problem, remains like a mountain no one tries any longer to climb.

There's something we haven't tried and it's a deeply religious practice. What I offer is not another political plan, but a simple meal. After all, gimmicks, marketing, programs, and meetings haven't worked. As Christians we are already gathered around a meal—the Last Supper—and we believe that Jesus is actually present in that meal and in every Eucharist held everywhere in the world on any day where two or three are gathered in his name. Take any meal where two or three people sit down to share food and wine and I say it is a shadow of the meal of Jesus. What if we will never deal with the race issue until we are breaking bread together in our homes?

When the church got its start, the new Christians spent a lot of time sharing meals with one another. New Testament scholars call this radical, open commensality. It's a term from anthropology. Commensality—from *mensa*, the Latin word for "table." It "means the rules of tabling and eating as miniature models for the rules of human relations. It means table fellowship as a map of economic discrimination, social hierarchy, and political differentiation." This is the image I will attempt to burn into our consciousness: The table in our homes is a miniature picture of our real values, beliefs, and relationships.

A cursory reading of the Gospels picks up the notion that Jesus will share a meal with anyone: social, moral, and political rejects. These are the people who, in high school, have to sit alone in the school cafeteria and are never allowed at the popular table, the cheerleader table, or the football players table. We should have learned from Jesus that we can't build up our righteousness by putting down the alleged unrighteous in our midst. We can tell that this was a major part of Jesus' life because his opponents berated him as a glutton, a drunkard, and a friend of tax collectors and sinners. He makes, in other words, no appropriate distinctions and discriminations like normal good people. This false name-calling is right there with the ones that claimed Jesus had no authority, that he was crazy, possessed by demons, and that he could not forgive sins. It's hard to know if the moralists thought his meal habits or being possessed of Satan was a higher criticism.

Recall the Pharisee's shock when Jesus didn't wash before eating. I once told my mother that Jesus didn't wash his hands before meals and this daughter of a preacher man, smiled and said, "Our Lord, unlike you, was without sin. Now wash your hands and your sins which are as scarlet shall be as white as snow." My mother's biblical knowledge was not a thing to be messed with by anyone.

As goes the table, so goes the culture. This is why the oft-repeated argument, "We are not racists," rings false. In our homes, around our table, we are as segregated as the 1950s. There might as well be a sign on the dining room door, "Whites Only." At best, we are recovering racists.

Remember the movie *Guess Who's Coming to Dinner*, starring Spencer Tracy, Katharine Hepburn, and Sidney Poitier? The film deals with a liberal family's discomfort at Joanna, their daughter's interracial marriage. They taught Joanna that all the races were equal. And they believed it until a man of another race was sitting at their table intending to marry their daughter. The plot of the movie unfolds around a meal and you can feel centuries of prejudice at play.

Guess who's coming to dinner? In the case of Jesus vs. the entire world of culture, religion, economics, and politics, there's no question: The poor are coming to dinner. The lepers are coming to dinner. The tax collectors (traitors to God and country) are coming to dinner. The Pharisees are coming to dinner.

In the truncated canon of many American liberal Christians, the meal stories of the Gospels are in the top ten beloved texts. Nothing is more thrilling to the liberal impulse in Christianity than Jesus consorting with sinners. This is why we can't allow liberals to control the entire narrative of the Gospels. New Testament scholar E. P. Sanders in *The Historical Figure of Jesus* says that Jesus never requires tax collectors and sinners to repent. All they had to do was accept him. John Dominic Crossan disagrees with Sanders. "It is almost like praising a serial killer for paying his traffic fines."[1]

Here we are looking down on people looking down on others and we have forgotten that God is looking down on us all. We think the good news is about the open-minded and the judgmental, but it's about the humble and the proud. Will Campbell once said he discovered that he was more prejudiced against the rednecks than the rednecks were prejudiced against blacks. Once you take what you consider the high moral ground, it is hard not to feel superior. The good news says the humble are in and the proud are out. The good news says that people who know they are not better, not more open-minded, not more moral than others, are in, and the people who think they are in the right and on the right side are most in danger.

One day Jesus went to dinner at the home of a Pharisee named Simon. During the meal there was a party crasher. Luke calls her "a woman in the city, a sinner." She comes to the table with an alabaster jar of ointment. She kissed Jesus' feet and anointed them. A deeply offended Simon: "How did this woman get past security?" He accuses Jesus of being a false prophet because Jesus doesn't know this woman is a sinner. In Simon's nasty world of good vs. bad, of limited categories, a true prophet would not allow a sinner to touch him. Simon thinks that knowledge consists of knowing who the bad people are. Simon stands for those who think that only the good people are in God's kingdom and the bad people are out—and Simon and the Pharisees say, "And of course we are the good ones." It is hard to resist the presumption that to have strong moral scruples, to oppose what you think is immoral, is good. To have "family values" is good. To be open-minded is bad. But Jesus doesn't seem to use these descriptions to separate the good from the bad. To be either, from the perspective of Jesus, is a problem.

But of all things, Jesus says, "Simon, do you see this woman? I entered your house; you gave me no water for my feet, but she has bathed my feet with her tears and dried them with her hair. You gave me no kiss, but from the time I came in she has not stopped kissing my feet. You did not anoint my head with oil, but she has anointed my feet with ointment." Simon violated all the rules of hospitality. "Therefore, I tell you, her sins, which were many, have been forgiven; hence she has shown great love." And he said to

1. Crossan, *Jesus*, Kindle ed., loc. 12338.

the woman, "Your faith has saved you; go in peace." The categories of Jesus: repentance, forgiveness, love, and faith.

Now, let's look at this same story through a different set of eyes.[2] In Mark's story emphasis is on the woman of the street: "Truly I tell you, wherever the good news is proclaimed in the whole world, what she has done will be told in remembrance of her." Why is this unnamed woman so important? Why does she get this amazing praise from Jesus? Why isn't she more important in the early church than she is? The male disciples of Jesus were told three times by Jesus that he would die and rise again.[3] The disciples never understood or accepted Jesus' impending death. But this unnamed woman—of all people—believes that Jesus is going to die and that unless his body is anointed now, it never will be. "Easter for her came early that year."[4] An unnamed woman, a woman from the street, embraces the good news; the "good guys" not yet.

That puts us at the table for the meal that matters the most: The Lord's Supper. When [Jesus] was at the table with them, he took bread, blessed and broke it, and gave it to them. Note the action: took, blessed, broke, and gave. These verbs indicate equal serving as the food is distributed to all. The host performs the role of servant. As amazing as this is, there's something more here. Remember the meal at the home of Mary and Martha. "There they gave a dinner for him. Martha served." Martha served because that was the rule: female hosting and serving. So at the Last Supper, "far from reclining and being served, Jesus himself, serves, like any housewife, the same meal to all, including himself."[5] By now, the religious elite, with their

2. Crossan points out that this woman believed the teaching of Jesus about his death before it, despite it, or even because of it.

3. See Mark 8:31–33, 9:30–32, and 10:32–37. Remember that Mark has a more critical views of the disciples than Matthew or Luke. "The disciples have never, as Mark sees it, understood or accepted Jesus' impending crucifixion. But now, in the home of Simon the leper, for the first time somebody believes that Jesus is going to die and that unless his body is anointed now, it never will be" (Crossan, *Jesus*, Kindle ed., loc. 3601). Crossan then makes the remarkable suggestion that this story may be "Mark" herself obliquely and indirectly signing her narrative. Ah, "Mark" a woman! We cannot ever be sure whether Mark was a woman or a man. We can, however, be absolutely sure that the author of this Gospel chose an unnamed woman for the supreme model of Christian faith—for the faith that was there before, despite, or even because of Jesus' death. Easter for her came early that year.

4. Ibid., loc. 3609.

5. Ibid., loc. 3388. Just in case anyone is still musing over the concept of an open table, let me tell you a story. A person gives a banquet and every invited guest RSVPs regrets. So the giver of the feast replaces the absent guests with anyone off the streets.

rule book for meals, thicker than an old Yellow Pages and just as obsolete, are like the lady looking at a new Buick, trying to grasp that it really is a Buick and saying, "Oh my!" Now radical egalitarianism and open commensality merge as good news!

And yet look at the church today. Some will not serve communion to the divorced and remarried. Some will not serve children or the unbaptized. Some will not serve any but their own members. "It is somewhat surprising that this image of Jesus sharing meals with marginal people ("sinners") handed on by Mark and Q seems to have had little influence in the early church."[6] Even Jesus had to repeat his lessons. Do you suppose it matters much that Jesus told Peter, "Feed my sheep"?

Imagine a meal at home with friends of different races. Will it bridge the chasm that still makes the issue of racism the most denied crime in our culture? When I suggested this to my liberal friends they balked at the idea and protested that our African American friends might not be comfortable having us in their homes. They also suggested that we can't "work" on race relations by announcing that we are having meals in order to "work" on race relations. Well, we are going to have meals together with some folks at Zion Baptist Church, a fellow American Baptist Church in Dayton that is African American. We are not going to "work" on race relations. We are going to break bread together and learn to be friends.

We shall overcome, but I believe it is time for the work of overcoming to take place in homes where white people and black people share meals with one another "with glad and generous hearts." After all, at the table we create friends and family. So lift your glass and fire up the grill! We are going to see one another at table!

"But if one actually brought in anyone off the street, one could, in such a situation, have classes, sexes, and ranks all mixed up together. Anyone could be reclining next to anyone else, female next to male, free next to slave, socially high next to socially low, and ritually pure next to ritually impure—lepers, the blind, the lame, the demon-possessed, a man named Legion, prostitutes, people with all manner of diseases, poor people. What a social nightmare that would be." (Ibid., loc. 1375.)

6. Donahue and Harrington, *The Gospel of Mark*, 104.

Choose Your Dayton

Rodney Wallace Kennedy

There are two cities named Dayton within spitting distance of one another: Dayton, Ohio—home of invention, imagination, science, and technology and Dayton, Tennessee—home of the Scopes Monkey Trial.

On the battleground of science and religion, it feels like the movie *Groundhog Day*. Every morning seems like a reconvening of the Scopes Monkey Trial in the summer of 1925 in Dayton, Tennessee. Carlyle Marney grew up a few miles from Dayton, Tennessee. He recalls that when word reached Dayton, Ohio that two of her sons had flown their airplane at Kitty Hawk, the town unbeliever said: "That's not so. Nobody can fly; nobody ever did; nobody ever will; and if they did, they wouldn't be anybody from Dayton, Ohio!"[1] Then Marney remarks of the fundamentalism in Dayton, Tennessee, where they "knew that fundamentalism wasn't dying; it never did die, it never would die, and if it did die it wouldn't do it in Dayton, Tennessee."[2] When William Jennings Bryan came to town to defend God and the Bible, he was opposed by Clarence Darrow, the devil. Marney says, "Everything is going to turn out right for Jesus. A great dragon-killer named Bryan has been sent by God Almighty to rescue your Bible, home, church, and sanity."[3] But Marney, even as an eight-year-old boy at the time, found himself secretly pulling for the dragon. The war thus started continues to this day.

The religious Right today fears evolution as much as it did in 1925 and brings the same tired arguments to the debate as they did then. Those on the Right stubbornly refuse to accept the plain truth that science undermines

1. Tompkins, *D-Days at Dayton*, 125.
2. Ibid.
3. Ibid., 126.

their literal interpretation of the Bible and they have spent the last century trying to discredit science.

The two main problems with creation science are that, as religious faith, it is patently false; and as science it is not science. The insistent argument that Christians can't believe in evolution comes from a constituency still locked in that courthouse in Dayton, Tennessee in 1925. They pound their Bibles while insisting that evolution is the work of the devil. They conveniently ignore that the larger Christian community has, almost from the beginning, accepted the findings of science about evolution.

Christians can participate fully in both the scientific and the religious community doing physics and math in a Wright Patterson lab and offering prayers and meditations in the sanctuary of a local church. We are not required to hold one worldview on Sunday and a different one on workdays.

There's room in the church for quarks and Quakers, for black holes and heaven, for science and faith, for the miracle of DNA and the vastness of the cosmos.

Christians have struggled with giving science its rightful due because science has demonstrated that a number of secondary and tertiary doctrines of the faith are simply false. For example, when Christians insist on defending non-truth as if it were truth (i.e., a six-day literal creation instead of a fifteen billion-year-old earth), there is conflict, but the conflict is between truth and non-truth, not between science and Christianity. A Christian is not obligated to defend a poetic, mythical story of creation as literal truth.

When early scientists suggested that the earth was round, the church clung to the flat earth theory because that's what the Bible claims. When Galileo demonstrated that the earth is not the center of the universe with the sun rotating around it, the church was there to slap him down. He was charged with heresy, threatened with torture and imprisonment, and made to denounce his new truth. Even today, you can see bumper stickers declaring: "God said it. I believe it. That settles it."

In fact, the church has been so wrong so often in its battle to debunk science that I automatically have serious doubts when the church makes pronouncements about scientific matters. I chose many years ago to dissent from church propaganda against science. One of the most remarkable things that the sciences have taught us about the universe is that it appears to possess all the capabilities it needs for organizing itself into a vast diversity of structures and forms. And it has been about this vigorous creativity and productivity for billions of years. Such a robustly equipped universe seems to upset many Christian people so they argue that some developments in organic life simply couldn't be the product of evolution.

I suggest that attention to what the universe supposedly cannot do is a basic denial of the robustness, the richness, and the fullness of God's gifts to the universe. When I consider the creation through a telescope, I am amazed at galaxies stacked on top of one another. When through the microscope I consider the creaturely cells that are continually knitted from generation to generation with double-helix of DNA, I can't but praise, *How majestic is your name, O Lord, in all the earth.*

This attack on science is producing negative results. More and more young people are accepting the anti-intellectual and anti-scientific arguments. In a world that has become intensely competitive in science and technology, this doesn't bode well for the nation.

I pray that other Christians will challenge the attack on science. We don't need religious theories of any kind masquerading as science. And no matter how hard creationists try to dress their theory in the robes of science, we are not prepared to grant it entrance into the realm of truth.

I suggest that we engage in a geographical metaphorical selection. Dayton, Tennessee, whether it deserves it or not, stands for the anti-scientific stance of some Christians. Dayton, Ohio, on the other hand, quite deservedly, has a reputation of being a veritable spawning ground of invention, science, technology, and academic excellence. We should pick Dayton, Ohio as our model for living in the new century and stop paying attention to those who want to take us back to the good old days.

Goodness Trumps Rights

Rodney Wallace Kennedy

I have an attraction to goodness. Maybe this is because I can be so mean and violent. I find that I have to pay attention to developing virtues that produce goodness in order to be good. Of course I am aware that there are "none that do good, not one," but this doesn't keep me from being part of the gigantic herd of humans trying to be "pretty good people" or people who "at least are not terrorists."

Goodness, good news, and God cannot be separated in the life of Jesus. They are the same. Goodness shouldn't be shy and reluctant among God's people. We need to be out there spreading the goodness. But we are a reticent bunch aren't we? Will Campbell once conceded to his imaginary African-American confessor, T. J., "You know, sometimes I get tired of working behind the scenes." T. J. responds, "Yeah, I guess it does get kind of crowded back there sometimes."

Isn't there something off key about Christians yammering about rights when we are slaves of Jesus? One way to tell that your faith has become more American than Christian is if you are always going on to doomsday about your rights. It feels like being trapped in a Flannery O'Connor story where hell is being one of those people in Georgia who has to sit and listen to your mother talk to you all day and all night, and you're ugly and peg-legged and must hear your mother go on about how dancing will send you to hell and stay out of the pool hall and all that degradation and manifold iniquity till doomsday.

Well, the way of Jesus was to be the servant. Will Campbell put the following conjecture in T. J.'s mouth: "When you think about it there's something pretty selfish about trying so hard to get my rights. Maybe the Christian thing to be doing is to be handing over the rights I already have.

Jesus said don't resist evil or persecution. Said if you take away my sweater to give you my coat. I'm telling you that as I read the Book, Brother Jesus is asking us to give up power, not get more. All those white cats under the big steeple churches, yeah they got power to give up. They got influence. And what's it good for? Go tell 'em to get rid of some of their power and influence. And when white folks drop their power, I'll tell mine to let it lie where it fell. Not to pick it up. Cause if they do they're in a peck of trouble."[1] We think that goodness derives from power, but goodness is not concerned with power. Still, we are engaged in typical power struggles. How often do we want our goodness to come from our power? Who among us would be willing to put down the power we have? Put down your power and then let goodness flow like honey from the rock. Jesus was offered all the power in the world by Satan and even as Satan tried to fit him with the purple robe of all that power, Jesus put it off like a country boy shucking corn. Instead of putting down one another, put down condescending and patronizing ways. Preachers face a lot of patronizing in the South. "You wouldn't believe our little preacher, he is the cutest thing, all those pretty curls. He is a ball of fire. He talks about our kids going to go to school with 'blacks.' He is a card, you know. He is a character; you know he is sort of our mascot. We love him and won't pay any attention to him. We don't believe all that, but it is nice to have the only preacher in town with a real PhD." The good people accepted the pride and power that came from having an educated pastor but completely rejected the preacher's message.

Who among us would practice some gospel and put down our power?[2] I think we are continually confusing power with goodness. Liberals often mistake secular altruism for God's goodness. The question is not how much power do we have, but how much goodness will we practice? If you want to be a difference maker in this world, don't seek the power but triple-down on goodness, acts of goodness, practices of goodness, sheer, complete, unexpected, second-mile goodness.[3]

---

1. Campbell and Goode, *Crashing the Idols*, 95–97.

2. In our fear-obsessed land, where politicians fall over one another to please the voters, our own Ohio legislature is considering allowing citizens over twenty-one to carry concealed weapons without a license and without training. Now, you may think that citizens armed to the teeth with guns is a healthy exercise of our second amendment rights. God bless you! But I think it is an unhealthy desire for power that attempts to give people the illusion of security.

3. Now I'm not talking about garden variety secular altruism. Liberals believe they are the good people and they are practicing goodness and they are, but it is not necessarily

We need to trust the gospel to do its work. Will Campbell wrote to the National Council of Churches' General Board of Social Concerns: "We just can't quite trust the power of the Gospel message. There just must be something we can add, some gimmick, some technique, some strategy. Just this once I wanted to rely only upon this [the gospel] and if it wasn't enough then let it not be enough. I am more and more convinced that it is enough if our witness to it is faithful."[4]

As Christians we are to live lives spreading the goodness of God. How much sheer goodness are we willing to produce? To learn to follow Jesus is the training necessary to become goodness. There may be nothing less Christian than insisting on our rights and using our power to get our way. To learn to live without rights, without certainty, without power, without protection, and without possessions is to follow Jesus.

---

the goodness of Jesus. Altruism is not the same being a Christian. Jesus told the rich young ruler to give away all his possessions. That is altruism. Then he said, "Come and follow me." That is Christianity. You can give away your goods without being a good person. The gift is actually a payment in return for power and privilege and the right to write the agenda for our nation. If you never look a gift horse in the mouth, you may discover that you backed the wrong horse. Charles Taylor says that we assume that the highest form of ethics is altruism. Good liberals are convinced that they are good people because they are filled with altruism instead of selfishness. This then becomes the highest virtue. Such a view is rooted in Christian spirituality but has now become a form of secular altruism. The love of God has been subtracted from altruism and this makes it something other than Christian. This suggests that we are pretty well convinced that we are good people but we no longer actually require God's help in this endeavor. If Christianity is simply altruism, being nice to others, accepting everyone, and not being prejudiced, then it hides from us that we have learned to live as if God does not exist.

4. Campbell and Goode, *Crashing the Idols*, 27.

Lies about the Bible and Gays

Rodney Wallace Kennedy

There are lies being told about the Bible and gays. By preachers who should know better, and probably do. They pose as Almighty God's spokesmen as if they were the second coming of Moses with the tablets of the Ten Commandments (nothing about gays in the Ten Commandments, by the way). They claim that their hearts are full of love for gays. Their serial abusive patterns mimic those of husbands who always insist, right after beating their wives, "But I love you." They clothe a blatantly political/social issue in pious rhetoric and peddle it as the essence of the gospel.

I'm not buying it. Even when they marshal all the Scripture they can dig up, they have only a half-dozen passages at best. They preach that God destroyed Sodom for sexual immorality, specifically homosexual immorality. That is a lie. There's no evidence that the men who stayed with Lot were sexually molested. If you want to actually know the sin of Sodom, go to Ezekiel 16:49–50: "This was the guilt of your sister Sodom: she and her daughters had pride, excess of food, and prosperous ease, but did not aid the poor and needy." The sin of Sodom: lack of hospitality. For those of you living by the creed, "The Bible says, I believe it; that settles it," you have some cognitive dissonance here.

I am particularly troubled by the insistence of preachers that the gay rights issue has nothing to do with the civil rights movement. There's a practical reason that good Christians don't want the gay movement to be parallel to the civil rights movement for African Americans. During the period leading up to the 1960s the people who supported racial equality and equal rights were persecuted by the good Christians. They were called socialists, communists, and troublemakers. They were condemned and castigated from the pulpits of prominent Southern Baptist churches. Today, the people supporting gay rights are receiving the same treatment from prominent pastors around the country. We are being called communists, socialists, liberals, and told that we are going against the Bible.

No wonder they don't want this to be a parallel situation. Well, let's set aside for the moment the argument that gay rights is not the same as civil rights. Instead let's concentrate on how gay rights supporters are being rhetorically treated by preachers and compare that to how civil rights supporters were rhetorically portrayed by preachers. Here the parallels are so striking as to seem practically the same. Perhaps the preachers protest too much. Their appeals to the Bible are ever present. The only thing that has changed is the exact verses that are quoted. Segregationist preachers quoted one set of verses and anti-gay preachers quote a different set of verses. Each group uses the Bible to condemn those with whom they are in disagreement.

Shame on these venom-spitting snakes of self-righteousness spewing their fear and anger, trying to control everybody with an impoverished reading of the Bible. If you insist on the enforcement of the entire Holiness Code of Leviticus (and not just that favorite prooftext in Leviticus 18), and the isolated references of St. Paul as your entire case against the equal treatment of gays, you have a hermeneutical crisis. You don't have enough gospel to save or damn the proverbial church mouse.

To my brothers determined to wreck entire denominations over this issue, I must say that you don't have enough evidence and the burden of proof is on you. You should pray about this some more, and when you get up off your knees, take a long and somber look at the wreckage of previous attempts to legislate moralism in America.

You are riding in a sinking ship. Justice, compassion, honesty, and equality will win in the long run. And your legacy? You will be welcomed into the gates of heaven with the knowledge that you gave your life to trying to keep the church purified from all those gay people. How tragic! From the great cloud of witnesses, you will have to watch as your progeny publicly confess your sin of mistreatment of gays and apologize for your angry condemnations. Fling open the church doors! Whosoever will may come!

A Baptism

Rodney Wallace Kennedy

The Jordan River goes into us on the day of our baptism and flows through our veins forever. Israel crossed Jordan into the Promised Land. Jesus was baptized there. Where was your Jordan? My Jordan was the Bayou D'Loutre —"The Looter"—a North Louisiana stream where we fished and hunted and went swimming. We'd been there for a thousand swims but it was different—clearer, colder maybe, swifter, deeper surrounded by Sunday dressed women and suited and tied men singing "Shall we gather at the river, the beautiful the beautiful river." On a Sunday afternoon in July, 1957, it beckoned as the Holy Land, the land of milk and honey, and we waded into the grainy-bottomed, clear water in a straight line. We whispered to one another, standing there, dressed in a white gown for the only time in our lives, and tried to trip one another under the water until the preacher whispered, "You boys, cut out your foolishness. You are on holy ground in holy water." Then the preacher took us by the hand, one by one, asked if we believed in Jesus, and pushed us beneath the waters with gentle hands while fish nibbled at our toes. We came up out of that water to the applause and shouted "Amens" of our congregation—everyone beaming from ear to ear because we once dead were now alive. Buried with Jesus in the waters of baptism, we were now raised to new life. Then we came out of the water and we sang "On Jordan's Stormy Banks I Stand." We had entered the river of life and we would never be the same again. Our sins had been washed away, ripped from us by the currents of the Jordan. We had been made cleansed and born again and sanctified and would go to heaven and nothing else really mattered in that holy moment.

Somehow it seems strange that Baptists, given our name and notoriety for sticking to baptism by immersion, have made so little of baptism. We have invented the "age of accountability" to counter our unwillingness to accept the validity of infant baptism. But that age is a moving target. Is it eight or twelve? How many children are baptized in Baptist churches each year under the age of five? And why do we put so much emphasis on baptism being when a child understands what she is doing? Isn't that too much trust in rationalism? Wouldn't a strong theology of baptism be the proper study for a Baptist?

Other than our steadfast opposition to infant baptism, we haven't really said much about baptism except to identify it as the symbolic rite that accompanies the personal confession of faith. Given the combination of individualism with the spectator passivity of a baptismal service, there's not much for us to do. Perhaps we can change this. If a church accepts the infant baptism of adults joining the congregation, that is the admission that the infant baptism is legitimate and a sign of grace. Does it then follow that having accepted those who were baptized as infants without requiring a re-baptism that we should take the next step and make infant baptism an option for our churches?

The baptism went deep enough to comfort and keep me to this day. Now all these fifty plus years later, I have added layers of meaning to that simple river baptism. Closing my eyes I can hear the Reverend Bevel Summers, in Flannery O'Connor's "The River": "If I baptize you, you'll be able to go to the Kingdom of Christ. You'll be washed in the river of suffering son, and you'll go by the deep river of life. Do you want that? You won't be the same again. You'll count."

The Doxology of Creation

Rodney Wallace Kennedy

I am in awe of creation—the vital, God-nourished, God-provided universe
capable of sustaining and flourishing life. For me the Bible doesn't have a
theology of creation; it has a doxology of creation. With the eyes of wonder,
I believe we behold the glory of creation. The accounts of creation in Scripture have such rhetorical, poetic power for me. Genesis 1 is a multi-stanza
praise song centered on the word "good." Genesis 1 offers us a stout defense
against the Gnosticism that tries to make us so spiritual as to be no earthly
good.

Over and over the song of praise is lifted in celebration of all that God
made was and is good. There is no reason to fear the material because it is
all God's creation waiting in eager longing. St. Paul tells us that "the creation waits with eager longing for the revealing of the children of God"
(Romans 12:19). The doxology reminds me that all creation—rocks and
rabbits, mountains and mountain lions, weeds and wind, Texas armadillos
and fire ants, Louisiana mosquitos and moles—longs for redemption. Not a
bad way to see the world: We exist as gift!

When creation is viewed as poetic power—as doxology—we are free
from the machinations of literalism, creationism, and scientism. Instead of
the flat prose of proofs, certainty, doctrines, scientific theories, and the like,
we are free to praise the Lord in all the earth. In one of the multiple stories
of creation in the Hebrew Scripture, Psalm 8 stands out as a primary example of the doxology of creation: "O Lord, our Sovereign, how majestic is
your name in all the earth! You have set your glory above the heavens. Out
of the mouths of babes and infants you have founded a bulwark because
of your foes, to silence the enemy and the avenger. When I look at your
heavens, the work of your fingers, the moon and the stars that you have

established; what are human beings that you are mindful of them, mortals that you care for them? Yet you have made them a little lower than God, and crowned them with glory and honor. You have given them dominion over the works of your hands; you have put all things under their feet, all sheep and oxen, and also the beasts of the field, the birds of the air, and the fish of the sea, whatever passes along the paths of the seas. O Lord, our Sovereign, how majestic is your name in all the earth!" Any theology that begins and ends with "O Lord, our Sovereign, how majestic is your name in all the earth" has my loyalty!

Since doxology properly belongs to the worship of the church, the doxology of creation is most clearly present in Eucharist: bread and wine. We can't get more fleshly, material, and basic than that. Through the bread and wine, the body and blood of Jesus, we become God's material body. Instead of some vague spiritualism that gives us a sense of salvation being all about us, we are ushered into the presence of God. What could be more essential than making God present in our midst? Creation turns out not to be a theological debate, but a doxological reality. There's no way we can keep God from being present throughout all of eternity no matter how we compute the age of the universe.

That being said, I am alert to every opportunity to celebrate God's real presence in all of creation. This is not to suggest some vague spiritualism as if church members playing golf on Sunday are experiencing a sacrament, but in the deeply connected sense of God being with us, for us, and among us. For example, once I stared into gray sky between Main Street skyscrapers. Sounds, not sight caused by head to lift and my eyes to behold. Honking I heard and not the angry honking of humans driving tons of steel and plastic in a hurry to get to a job they probably didn't like. These sounds were lyrical, with notes of the miraculous echoing through space. There before my eyes, flying low and in a perfect V was eight Canada geese looking for all the world as large as jumbo jets. Surely the wind on my cheeks came from the beat of their massive wings. I beheld the jarring contradiction of wild geese and human engineering sharing space. Surely this was a no-fly zone. And yet they seemed so at home in our wild world, so natural, seemed to be crying this was their world before it was ours. As if the steel and glass were just different kinds of trees, they swooped down Main, turned left on Monument and hovered over First Baptist Church, circled once, and stuck their landing in the Great Miami with the elegance of an Olympic gymnast. Breath left me; speech defied me. Life stood nearly still, silent as if my brain had an app for slow motion review. My turning to follow them down the street seemed to capture all time in this one moment. Canada geese flying in perfect alignment down Main Street—a gift from God, a gift received in wonder, love, and praise. Now, every day of the winter solstice I walk down Main Street toward the river with one eye on the sky, but if I never see them again the gift will always remain. May the Holy Spirit always give us ears to hear and eyes to see the glory, splendor, beauty, and majesty of all God's creation.

We Have a Jordan to Cross Again and Again

Rodney Wallace Kennedy

The baptismal scene in the back of the baptistery at the Antioch Baptist Church was a faded larger than life painting of the Jordan River—deep, wide, bright blue water. Later I would be told that the actual Jordan looked nothing like the painting. Yet, in my metaphorical imagination the Jordan is more like that picture than the reality. The Jordan is everywhere. St. Gregory of Nyssa wrote: "For indeed the river of grace flows everywhere. It spreads over the whole earth and flows into Paradise." Jean Danielou elaborates: "The Jordan is the mythical river, which encircles the whole world and is contrasted with the mythical rivers of Paradise. The Jordan is the source of Baptism . . . . the idea found in all Christian liturgies that all baptismal water is the Jordan . . . . Jordan, as the frontier between the world of the sense and the spiritual world."[1]

The Jordan is there when people are oppressed. Israel, up from Egypt, fresh from the fleshpots of slavery, stood at the Jordan and failed to cross. She stood on the edge of promise and couldn't muster the courage to cross over. The Jordan always flows in the direction of people who are oppressed and fearful. Crossing the Jordan means freedom and liberation. For escaped slaves prior to the Civil War, the Ohio River was the Jordan. "I'll meet you in the morning / when you reach the promised land / on the other side of the Jordan / for I'm bound for the promised land."

Whatever holds us back in fear—that's our Jordan. Christians are afraid of so much in our nation and this fear is driving them to stand on the banks of the Jordan, unwilling to go forward, unwilling to cross over. They want to go back, turn back the clock, to a simpler time, an innocent time, a mythical time that actually has never existed. I am convinced that fear is the

---

1. Danielou, *From Shadows to Reality*, 272.

primary message of the powers and principalities in America. The drums are beating, the fires are burning, the politicians are howling—in America it's Halloween every day. Billions of dollars have been spent on campaign advertising telling us that the other candidates are a collection of low-life, lying, stealing, and conniving idiots without enough sense to come in out of the rain. The Truth in Advertising police need to arrest all the political consultants and ad writers, handcuff them, and haul them off to prison.

The opposite of all this fear-mongering is the gospel of Jesus. He too came down to the Jordan to be baptized. He took his place with us in the Jordan to lead us to the promised land. Do not be afraid. Let not your hearts be troubled. Lift up weak knees. Come to the throne of grace and find help in time of need. There's our politics and here's the gospel and they are not the same. Whatever holds us back from greatness, from vision, from taking on the powers and the principalities, that's our Jordan. But God never intended the Jordan to be an obstacle.

PART II: Selected Sermons

The Power of Weakness
and the Weakness of Power

Ephesians 6: 10–20; Mark 10: 35–45

Twenty-first Sunday after Pentecost, October 21, 2012

KYLE CHILDRESS

One of the places I look to see the church being the church is Birmingham in the spring and summer of 1963. It is not the only place to look but it is one place where the church stood up and acted like the church is supposed to act. In 1961 and '62 the victories against the powers of death, or what the Apostle Paul calls the principalities and powers, had been few and far between. But by 1963 Martin Luther King, Fred Shuttlesworth, and a host of others in the African-American church went head to head with the powers, represented by Public Safety Commissioner Bull Connor.

By that spring, it looked as if the powers of racism and segregation might win once again. Bull Connor had more jail space than the civil rights workers had people. Until the youth got involved. The Birmingham powers of death no longer were facing 50 people a day, but 500 and 1,000, every day, day after day. They were filling all the jails in the entire state of Alabama. One Sunday afternoon, 2,000 young people came out of worship in Birmingham's New Pilgrim Baptist Church to march. The police were shocked. How much longer was this going to go on? How many more were they going to have to arrest? It looked as if the civil rights workers kept coming up with more and more and more people. On this Sunday, the line of young people was five blocks long. Along the way, on the sidewalk, mothers and fathers, grandmothers and grandfathers sang hymns, quoted Scripture, prayed, and shouted and cried to the young people, "Don't give up baby, God is with you!" They cried because in those days, a young black person going to the white jail had a very good chance of never being seen again. So here they were sending their children and grandchildren to jail to the prospect of torture and even death. When the long line of young people approached the barricade of police and dogs and firemen and firehoses, Bull Connor himself walked out to confront them, shouting for the firemen to turn on the hoses and for the police to let loose the dogs.

The line of young people drew close—right up, face to face with Connor and the firemen and police. Then they knelt and prayed and young Rev. Charles Billups stood and shouted, "Turn on your water! Turn loose your dogs! We will stand here 'til we die!" For a few moments no one knew what was going to happen, but then Billups and the young people stood up and began to walk forward. There was tension, hesitation, and then the firemen and police parted for them to pass. Onlookers recalled it was just as the Red Sea had parted for the Children of Israel.[1]

For over thirty-two years of serving as a pastor, twenty-three of them here, I've been asking myself, how do you form and nourish a church that produces young people like that? And how can we be a church that grows and trains all kinds of people who can discern when it is time to stand and then have the courage to stand?

The Apostle Paul, while in prison wrote, "Be strong in the Lord and in the strength of his power. Put on the whole armor of God … For our struggle is not against the enemies of blood and flesh, but against the rulers, against the authorities, against the cosmic powers of this present darkness, against the spiritual forces of evil in the heavenly places. Therefore, take up the whole armor of God, so that you may be able to withstand on that evil day, and having done everything, to stand firm" (Eph 6:13).

In our Gospel reading this morning from Mark, brothers James and John, known among the other disciples as the "Sons of Thunder" for their audacity and quick temper, came up to Jesus and said, "Teacher, when you win the election, when you take charge, we want you to appoint us to high positions of power so we can help you get things done and run these mean Romans out" (Mark 10:35–37). "They've beaten us down and we're sick and tired of it. It's time for them to get some of their own medicine and you're just the one to give it to them. So when you win, appoint us to some positions of power."

1. Branch, *Parting the Waters,* 768.

Jesus says, "You don't know what you're talking about. You don't even know what I'm talking about. My way of ruling is by suffering servanthood, not by coercive power."

The rest of the disciples heard James and John's request and were mad at them and jealous. So Jesus called all of them together and said, "You know that among the Gentiles their rulers lord it over them. Their rulers wield coercive power in order to rule. That's the way they do things. But it is not that way among us. We live a different way. Whoever wants to be great must be a servant, for I came not to be served but to serve, even to give my life" (Mark 10:41–45). Throughout Jesus' ministry, everywhere he went, he taught and preached and showed what his kind of servant-rule looked like. When Jesus called his disciples together, he gave them this new way of life to live. A new way to deal with offenders—by forgiving them. A new way to deal with violence—by non-violent suffering. A new way to deal with money—by sharing it. A new way of relationships between woman and man, parent and child, people of different races, gay and straight people, people who are different in all kinds of ways, in which there can be seen a radical new vision of what it means to be human. This new way is called the kingdom of God, the reign of God, the commonwealth of God, the beloved community.

This is the new kind of servant-ruler Jesus showed us when he healed the sick, served the poor, included the outcasts, listened to women and poor widows, lifted up children, ate with sinners, and challenged the religious leaders. This new kind of servant-ruler threatened the social order, was a menace to the political order, disrupted the economic order and challenged the conventional order. All so he could show us God's new order. And it is this new way of God to which we are invited to become citizens and participants through baptism. And in baptism we are formed into a people, a community that seeks to practice what Jesus preached. A community that the New Testament calls church.

Now there's a lot that this means. Part of what I'm saying is a stark reminder of how the conventional church in this country, for the most part, has fallen away from the call of the God we know in Jesus. The church in the US often tends to side with the powerful and not the powerless. We are more interested in ruling than serving.

But it also means that if we join Jesus in this way of living, then we begin to see differently from those on top. We see from the bottom; from the perspective of those who are ground down, beaten down, worn out, in poverty, and in poverty of spirit—you know what poverty of spirit is? It is when the person in poverty begins to believe deep down inside that he or she really is less than human. So we learn to see from the point of view of those who are diminished, defeated, in despair. We see from the position of weakness.

It also means that we learn to trust the power of weakness and to recognize the weakness of power. With power there are some things that cannot be accomplished. Sort of like swatting flies with a baseball bat. The powerful tend to think one-dimensionally: take over and rule. But those of us who are weak do not have that option so we have the freedom to try creative ways to live out this kind of life.

Much of the time, we are able to serve God, serve others, and serve God's good creation without a lot of conflict. But there are times when the Way of Jesus, the Way of life, collides with the ways of the powers of death. Sometimes, we find ourselves in a place like Peter and John in Acts 4, when they were facing the religious powers who were telling them to shut up or else, and they said, "Whether it is right in God's sight to listen to you rather than to God, you must judge; for we cannot keep from speaking about what we have seen and heard" (Acts 4:19-20). Sometimes we have to make a stand.

Sometimes to keep those without power from being destroyed or hurt or diminished, and this includes God's creation, we have to make a stand and say we're no longer going to cooperate with this. But we're going to make our stand in the Way of the suffering servant Jesus. We do so non-violently and in humility, and even in fear and trembling.

I speak to you partly from my own experience of non-violent civil disobedience in 1985 opposing the Reagan Administration policy of supporting the contras in Nicaragua. I was arrested in Washington in front of the State Department building for blocking the driveway, along with about fifty other clergy. I spent five days in jail. And I've participated in numerous other protests, usually over war but also over homelessness issues, and especially I'm now supporting our Keystone XL pipeline blockaders. I'm also speaking with the help of farmer and writer Wendell Berry who has committed non-violent civil disobedience three times: once for blocking the construction of a nuclear power plant near his farm and twice while opposing mountain-top removal by the coal industry.[2]

2. Berry, "About Civil Disobedience," 103–9.

And finally, I'm dipping into the teaching and wisdom of the church, which remembers all the way back to the time of Pharaoh in Exodus 1, when he commanded all the Hebrew boy babies be killed upon birth, and the Bible says that the Hebrew midwives, Shiphrah and Puah, "feared God; they did not do as Pharaoh commanded, but they let the boys live" (Exod 1:17).

Even with a long and rich tradition of the people of God standing against legal authority we do so with humility. Part of our humility is because it is scary to oppose legal authority. It's not fun and once you do it, you discover there is no romance in it. It is an act of last resort. Only after everything else has been tried are we willing to commit non-violent civil disobedience.

It's hard. It is hard because always, always we are to love our enemies, no matter how irresponsible or uninformed or corrupt or wrong we believe they are. Those we oppose are not the people who arrest us. The powers we face are larger than individual people. These folks, like us, are caught in webs that are bigger than they are. Sometimes they are even enmeshed in evil. But we know that the line between good and evil goes right down the middle of each of our hearts so we have deep humility. The difference is that perhaps we recognize it and they don't. Our job is to make a witness (pointing to the Way of Jesus, the Way of love and life) so we show them that there is another way; there is a way out. Some folks we face who are the arresting officers are working double-shifts, or they're working for Trans-Canada on the side so they can make ends meet. We want to behave in such a way that they sense that our arms are open and big enough to include them, too.

It is hard and scary because we stand without power. We are non-violent and therefore we open our lives up to possible violence. We can be hurt; we'll likely go to jail and face criminal charges, fines and a possible criminal record.

It is hard and scary because in the short-term we feel like what we do may be useless. Occasionally, like the young civil rights activists of 1963 in Birmingham, jails can be filled and the unjust legal system will break down, prompting the desired change. But most of the time, we are outnumbered, overwhelmed, and under-funded. Most of the time we will lose.

But we lose only in the short-term. It is essential that we learn to see for the long haul. We do not have undue optimism when it looks like we're winning because we know that this is a long haul battle and things shift and can change. But we also learn to hope when it looks like there is no reason for hope. This is why it is so important to have a spiritual life rooted in the God who sustains us over the long haul. We are here to stand and to stand when everyone else gives up and goes home. We want to put our spiritual roots down so deeply that we can out-stand the pipeline. One of these days, if we can keep standing, the pipeline people might very well give up and go home. But it is going to be a long, long stand.

I remember a group of Mennonites during the late sixties who were marching seven times around a nuclear missile base and then blowing toy trumpets, in imitation of Joshua marching around the city of Jericho. After marching seven times and blowing their toy trumpets, a reporter said, "You know the walls are not coming down." And one of the Mennonites replied, "Oh, they will. They will. One day they will." We have a long haul vision and we must learn how to be sustained over the long haul.

This why the Apostle Paul urges the little church in Ephesus to put on the whole armor of God, deepen their lives in God, because we're in a battle and it is long and hard.

This is hard and scary. So we do this as an act of prayer. Standing against injustice is done with humility ultimately because we are standing before God in prayer. Without God's very present help, we will not stand and things will not change.

James 5:16 says, "The prayer of the righteous is powerful and effective." And I believe this is true of acts of non-violent civil disobedience when done in humility before God. When we stand as an act of prayer, remember that there is much more going on than simply what we can see.

Old peace activist A. J. Muste once stood day after day, all by himself, outside the gate of a nuclear base, holding a sign that said, "Ban the Bomb." After several days, someone said to him, "You know you're not going to change them." Muste said, "I know. But I can keep them from changing me."

Muste standing alone was an act of defiance—to keep the powers of death from changing him. It was an act of prayer and an act of faith in the God who is greater than all the powers of death put together. It was an act of hope that God would use his solitary act of fidelity to bring about change.

Wendell Berry tells of an occasion back in 1966 when he attended a hearing in the Kentucky state capital over strip mining for coal. There were perhaps fifteen people present whose homes and land were damaged or threatened by the coal mining. That day there was no "demonstrating" but those folks were there in protest nonetheless. One man in the group was dressed neatly in a summer suit. Wendell eventually introduced himself to the man, whom he discovered was a lawyer over in Eastern Kentucky. The lawyer was not there representing anyone but himself. Wendell said, "Then why are you here?" He replied, "I want to be on the side of right."

For Wendell, and for me, over the long haul, that is enough. To be on the side of right. Can you stand because you are on the side of right?

In 1965 Martin Luther King stood on the steps of the Alabama State Capital speaking in favor of voting rights, seeking to open up voting rather than limit it. He said; "I know you are asking today, 'How long will it take?'"

"I come to say to you this afternoon, however difficult the moment, however frustrating the hour, it will not be long, because truth crushed to earth will rise again."

"How long? Not long, because no lie can live forever."

"How long? Not long, because you shall reap what you sow." . . .

"How long? Not long, because the arc of the moral universe is long, but it bends toward justice."

Can you stand on that? Can you stand over the long haul?

Like Dr. King, like the children in Birmingham in 1963, and like so many others who have sought to stand in the Way rooted in the God we know in Jesus, we can stand here 'til we die.

In the name of the Father, the Son, and the Holy Spirit. One True God, Mother of us all. Amen.

*This sermon was preached in a congregation of less than 100 people, of whom about 20 were members of the Tar Sands Pipeline Blockade, who had been in church every Sunday for over a year and would continue to be in church for several months after this, when they were not in jail, arrested for protesting and attempting to block the construction of the TransCanada Keystone XL Pipeline by tree sitting and chaining themselves to heavy construction equipment. Members of our congregation acted in support of these blockaders.

Who's Arresting Whom?*

John 18: 1–12 (33–38)

Christ the King Sunday, November 25, 2012

KYLE CHILDRESS

This morning is Christ the King Sunday. It is the last Sunday of the Christian calendar, the climax, before we begin a new year next week with the First Sunday of Advent. Our calendar ends with a bang, not a whimper. It ends with the assertion that Jesus Christ rules!

This morning our lesson is from John 18. John's Gospel is full of layers of meaning, symbol, metaphor, analogy, paradox, and irony. And today we get lots of irony.

Jesus and his disciples have been in the upper room sharing the last supper where Jesus also washed his disciples' feet, and then prays a long prayer. Then they went out, crossed over the Kidron Valley, to the Garden of Gethsemane. Roughly speaking that would be about like going from here down Austin Street across University and up to say, the Cotton Patch Restaurant. It's about the same distance across the Kidron Valley.

Meanwhile, Judas, the betrayer, leads a contingent of soldiers, Temple police, priests from the Temple, and Pharisees to the Garden looking to arrest Jesus. But it's not simply a contingent; we're not talking about 3 or 4 soldiers coming to arrest one man. The word we translate as contingent is the word for a cohort of Roman troops, which was about 500 soldiers. Down in verse 12, the word we translate as officer or captain, *chiliarchos*, means the leader of 1,000 men. So we're not sure, but it sounds as if anywhere between 500 and 1,000 Roman soldiers come marching up to arrest Jesus.

Of course, that's not all. There were also Temple police with them. Now the Temple Police were priests, religious types, who were also into security.

We don't know how many but there were enough to be mentioned. And also chief priests from the Temple and Pharisees—remember that priests from the Temple and Pharisees, who were in the synagogues, didn't like one another. And they didn't like Romans either. But here, they join forces in their effort to get this threatening rabbi, Jesus of Nazareth.

So, as best as we can tell, there are over 500 soldiers coming along with a bunch of religious leaders and preachers—church and state joining up with one another. Mark my word, when church and state get mixed up with one another it is never, never a good thing. It is bad for the state and it is bad for the religion. What always happens is the state thinks it can use religion to further its goals while religion thinks it can use the state to coerce its goals. Both church and state are perverted.

One of the many things this story tells us is that Jesus was not brought down by atheism and anarchy. He was brought down by law and order allied with religion. Beware of those who claim to know the mind of God and who are prepared to use violence, if necessary, to make others conform. Beware of those who cannot tell God's will from their own. Temple police are always a bad sign. When preachers start wearing guns and hanging out with the sheriff's office, watch out. When church ushers start arming themselves on Sunday morning, beware!

But that's not all. They are armed to the teeth—500 soldiers and preachers with swords and spears, shields and body armor. They have their riot gear, their tear gas and pepper spray. A helicopter is circling overhead. They're not fooling around. Like one deputy, badge number 514, said last week before pepper spraying the crowd at the pipeline blockade, "Let's go make a point." They're not simply going to make an arrest; not with 500 troops in riot gear. They're going in to make a point about anyone who dares to challenge the authority of Caesar, the emperor of Rome. They're going in with shock and awe.

Finally, they're all carrying torches and lanterns. They're using spotlights, flares, bright flashlights and any other artificial light they can find in order to see the True Light of the world. Irony indeed.

Five hundred soldiers and preachers, armed to the teeth, with lights everywhere. What are they afraid of? Who's in charge here? And why are they threatened?

All of this force, all of this power to arrest one man? And it's not like he had an army of seasoned soldiers or trained revolutionaries with him. The rag-tag disciples of Jesus were all pretty young. Jesus was about thirty-three and scholars tell us that Peter was perhaps around twenty-five or twenty-eight. The other disciples were most likely in their early 20s and late teens. And John, the beloved disciple, was the youngest and scholars say that he was about fourteen or fifteen. Plus, remember their backgrounds—fishermen, a tax collector, assorted this and that. And that's just the men that we know about. We also know that the many women who followed were also young, although in this story of the arrest in the Garden, we don't know if any women were present or not. We do know that it is the women who stay when Jesus is executed on the cross, while all the men flee. So probably Jesus had these dozen men plus another six or eight women, all of them young, and all of them had quit what they were doing, had given up everything to join the Jesus movement.

Anyway you figure it, Jesus and these disciples should not be threatening to the powers. Or are they? And why are they?

Five hundred heavily armed troops and a bunch of pistol-packing preachers, with all the lights they can muster show up in the Garden of Gethsemane—which by the way is not that large a space. The Garden was about the size of our church parking lot. So it had to be a little crowded when all 500 or 600 showed up looking for this one man, Jesus.

They fan out ready for battle. Some officers are checking license plates on all the cars in the Garden parking lot, while others are videoing everyone present, including those standing nearby. Have no doubts, the powers are taking names and checking them twice. They want to keep up with who has been naughty or nice.

The irony continues. The mass of troops march into the Garden and Jesus steps forward to meet them, and asks, "For whom are you looking?"

The irony shifts into satire. When the troops come into the Garden and Jesus steps forward to meet them, the front line of officers stop abruptly and everyone behind them runs into the soldiers in front and you get this massive domino effect. They come to get Jesus but they don't even know him when he steps forward. "For whom are you looking?" And they answer, "Jesus of Nazareth."

Jesus answers, "I am he." The more accurate translation would be "I am." These are the same words that go all the way back to the Old Testament to Moses tending sheep in the backside of the desert in Exodus 3, when he meets God through the burning bush. When Moses asks for God's name, God replies with "I am." More than a name; it's a verb—the verb to be. God was, God is, God will be.

In John, Jesus says, "I am." I am the Bread of Life; I am the Vine; I am Living Water; I am the Way, the Truth, and the Life… I am.

When Jesus utters, "I am," the whole cohort of soldiers and officials, preachers, and the rest with all their armor and arms, torches and lanterns, step back and fall to the ground!

What's going on here?

Remember that Paul says in Philippians, "Therefore God also highly exalted him and gave him the name that is above every name, so that at the name of Jesus every knee should bend, in heaven and on earth and under the earth, and every tongue should confess that Jesus Christ is Lord" (Phil 2:9–11).

In Colossians, Paul says, "He has rescued us from the powers of darkness … He is the image of the invisible God, the firstborn of all creation; for in him all things in heaven and on earth were created, things visible and invisible, whether thrones, or dominions or rulers or powers—all things have been created through him and for him. He himself is before all things, and in him all things hold together … For in him all the fullness of God was pleased to dwell, and through him God was pleased to reconcile to himself all things …" (Col 1:13–20).

The powers don't like it; and whether they expect it or not, when they hear "I am" from Jesus, they fall to the ground. The powers come face to face with the One who is ruler of the universe.

Speechless, they gather themselves; they get up. But Jesus must ask them again, "For whom are you looking?" Once again, they say, "Jesus of Nazareth." And Jesus says, "I told you, I am. So if you are looking for me, let these other people go."

Who's arresting whom? Who's in charge? Who rules?

At Jesus' command the powers release the disciples and arrest Jesus. The so-called rulers of this world, with all their authority and power, cannot even do their own work. Jesus must do it for them. So they release everyone else they've grabbed and cuffed, and they seize Jesus.

This scene is so ludicrous that it's almost out of a scene of the Keystone Kops (pun intended). Except it involves violence, pain, and the eventual torture and death of Jesus, an innocent man.

Why do we have this story? And why does John tell it? It's serious business but it is told with irony and satire? It is told with foolishness.

First of all, remember that the audience for John's Gospel is not the high and mighty, the rich and powerful. The people who were listening to this story from John being read to them were small bands of believers, huddled around a few lamps and candles in someone's home or in catacombs, tunnels under the city of Rome. They were hiding out from the powers. They were persecuted, wanted. They were outnumbered, overwhelmed, disheartened, and in despair.

And John writes for them of Jesus' own arrest, showing them that the powers of death do not have all the power. Indeed, ultimately the powers are supposed to be in the service of God. They are to be servants of goodness and peace. That's why they were created in the first place. But they have rebelled against God, trying to live and rule for themselves. And they think that anyone who refuses to knuckle under to their rule, must be crushed.

To encourage the scattered, small, rag-tag followers of Jesus, John unmasks the powers. He exposes them and shows them to all of us for what they truly are. And the way he does that is by using irony and satire. And the powers of death are not in charge. Jesus Christ is ultimately in charge.

Using foolishness and humor, satire, and irony is a time honored method by those considered weak against the powers of death. It is one way we punch a hole in their balloons of pretension.

The Apostle Paul says in Colossians that Jesus "disarmed the Powers and made a public example of them, triumphing over them" (2:15). That's what John is showing us. Jesus is exposing the powers and disarming them. The powers want to convince us that they are large and in charge and that they know and serve all that is important, good, just, and right.

But Jesus shows them up for who they truly are. They don't serve all that is good and just and right. And they don't have the power they like to think they have. The powers are not the rulers; Jesus Christ is Lord and Ruler.

The psalmist says, "The earth is the Lord's and the fullness thereof; the world and those who dwell therein" (Ps 24:1). The earth is the Lord's; it does not belong to TransCanada. It does not belong to the coal companies; it does not belong to Exxon. It doesn't belong to Wall Street or to Washington or Austin. It belongs to the Lord. And as servants of the Lord we are called to care and serve for the earth and all its inhabitants.

One of the most ludicrous, foolish things I've seen in a long time was last Monday at the west park of Lake Nacogdoches when Vicki, Kerry, Marilyn R., Maya, Maggie, and Marilyn E. dressed up in foolish grandmother clothes and joined another five or six others in parodying the tar sands pipeline. They dressed up as Nacogdoches' version of the Raging Grannies (originated in Canada as a foolish way of protesting war and destruction of the environment) and sang a song about the pipeline to the tune of "She'll Be Coming Around the Mountain."

While they sang, we were all kept under surveillance by two police cruisers with two officers in each cruiser. One cruiser kept an eye on the old ladies singing while the other recorded and ran a check on every license plate in the parking lot.

Of course, one of those Raging Grannies, who happens to be a real seventy-five year old grandmother, Jeanette S., later was pepper-sprayed by a zealous deputy for not getting out of the way fast enough.

How ironic that old ladies threaten a pipeline. How ironic that 500 heavily armed soldiers seek to arrest one man, Jesus, and can't even do that without his direction.

How ironic that Jesus our king rules not by power but in weakness; not by fear but by love; not by coercion but by forgiveness and grace. Jesus Christ rules not from a throne but from the cross.

In the name of the Father, the Son, and the Holy Spirit. One True God, Mother of us all. Amen.

*This sermon, preached about a month after the "The Power of Weakness" sermon, followed a week of non-violent civil disobedience and resistance to the Keystone XL Pipeline as well as foolish lampooning of the powers that be. Six active attendees of our congregation had been arrested and others had been pepper-sprayed by deputy sheriffs clearing the way for pipeline construction to continue.

We Can Breathe

Acts 2:1–21; John 14:25–27, 20:19–23

Pentecost Sunday, May 24, 2015

KYLE CHILDRESS

Not being able to breathe is much on my mind these days. I went through a sleep study a few weeks ago and discovered that during the night I can't breathe. I have sleep apnea, that condition in which my breathing stops multiple times during the night, multiple times every hour of the night. My breathing stops and therefore my oxygen stops, my body and lungs and heart have to strain and work harder, rather than resting and renewing. So I partially awaken to catch my breath, even though I'm not aware of waking. And as a further result, I never really get a good night's sleep. I do not have much of that really important REM sleep which is essential to full rest, full renewal, full regeneration that should come as a result of good breathing and good sleep.

I had the sleep study because I found myself perpetually tired, exhausted, fatigued, and so on. I have found myself discouraged, more than usual. All because I can't breathe like I should.

Of course, I now have a CPAP machine, which I am only now beginning to learn to use. I have not yet become "compliant" with it (as the language of the respiratory therapist says) so I have not yet begun to receive the benefits of restored breathing and new vitality.

Not being able to breathe is much on our minds these days.

Eric Garner, in Staten Island, New York said, "I can't breathe!" eleven times on camera, as he was held in an illegal chokehold by police officers, with his hands cuffed behind his back. Eleven times, as he was on the ground, face-down, pleading "I can't breathe!"

The only response from the police officer was "F--- your breath!"

Even after he went limp, and the officers released the chokehold, after he was unconscious on the ground, face-down for seven minutes—no one checked on him, no one checked to see if he was breathing. EMT's were called and eventually tried CPR on him. And at the emergency room of the hospital he was pronounced dead upon arrival. The coroner ruled it a homicide but the grand jury made no indictments.

Not being able to breathe is much on our minds these days.

Breathing is essential. It is life. When we can't breathe we die.

John tells us that on the evening of that first Easter Day the disciples were gathered behind closed and locked doors. Some of them had been out that morning to the cemetery where Jesus had been buried and had seen the open tomb. Some of the women came back and said that Jesus was resurrected and Mary Magdalene had even talked with him, but it was so outlandish that no one could really be sure. Besides, soldiers were everywhere outside, the city was tense, the religious and political authorities were hunting for anyone still stirring up trouble, and the SWAT Teams and riot squads were on full alert.

So the disciples made no loud noises, provided no reason to call attention that anyone might be present in that small room. No lights, no candles, no movements. No talking, just whispers. Quiet, dark, closed, locked-down —don't even breathe … It was as if the disciples were almost choking on their fear, choking on the quiet, choking in the closed, hot, stuffy room. You could almost hear the drops of sweat hitting the floor.

And all of a sudden Jesus himself walks into the room. Holy Son of God! "Peace, brothers and sisters," he says loudly! And then he shows them his wounds from the cross. Everyone gets excited and Jesus says again, "Peace. Peace, brothers. Peace, sisters. Just as God has sent me, I'm sending you." Then he did a remarkable thing: He breathed on them and said, "Receive the Holy Spirit."

He had tried to prepare them. Back four nights before, in that same room, when they had all shared a meal together and Jesus had washed their feet, he had told them that God would send the Holy Spirit, the Comforter, the Advocate to them, who would remind them all of what Jesus had been saying. And sure enough, Jesus kept his promises.

This was no small thing that Jesus breathed on them and gave them the Holy Spirit.

For John, the one who recorded all of this, Jesus is the Word, the Living Word. John begins, "In the beginning was the Word, and the Word was with God, and the Word was God. He was in the beginning with God. All things came into being through him and without him not one thing came into being. What has come into being in him was life, and the life was the light of all people" (John 1:1–4).

In and through Jesus, the Living Word, there is New Creation. John is echoing Genesis. Remember the original Creation: In the beginning God created the heavens and the earth. It goes on over in chapter 2 where it says, "Then the Lord God formed the human from the ground (from the humus), and God breathed into his nostrils the breath of life; and the human became a living being" (Gen 2:7).

Rabbis over centuries have commented that this is the essence of the worship of God: inhaling God's breath, and exhaling into the world. Worship is breathing. Life is breathing. Having life and worshiping God are one and the same.

John is telling us that Jesus is breathing upon the disciples, just like the original Creation, so they are re-created in and through him. The breath of God is the breath of life. Without the breath of God, there is death.

Not being able to breathe is much on our minds these days.

You can make a case that the whole Bible is the story of the people of God learning to breathe, trying to find breathing space, and the story of God helping them breathe, cleanly, clearly, fully with deep and complete breaths. As Jesus says, "I have come that you may have life and have it abundantly" (John 10:10). You have to breathe in order to have life.

The most formative and central story of the Old Testament is the Exodus story. The people of God are slaves in Pharaoh's Egyptian Empire and Pyramid Scheme. They are worked 24/7 all the time, every day, every week, every month, every year, every generation to make the quota of bricks determined by Pharaoh's managers, to make that bottom-line, to make that next goal, and if they exceed the margin today, tomorrow has to be better. It never ends. The Bible says that the Israelites "groaned" in their slavery under Pharaoh. They cried out to Pharaoh, "We can't breathe!" But Pharaoh said, "F--- your breath!" So they groaned to God, "We can't breathe!" And it says, "God heard their groaning … God looked upon the Israelites, and God paid attention to them" (Exod 1:23–25).

Moses said to Pharaoh, "Thus says the Lord God of Israel, 'Let my people go, so that they may go three days out into the wilderness and worship the Lord God'" (Exod 5:1–3). In other words, "Let my people have some breathing room. Let them worship the God who gives life and gives breath."

Finally, after all of the plagues and all of the trials and tribulations and intervention of God, the Israelites are set free in order to go to a new place where they can have some breathing room and worship the God of life and breath.

This is the biblical story. In the Old Testament it is slavery and freedom in the land of promise. In the New Testament it is the cross and resurrection. But the story is always about moving from death to life, from being choked to death, to being able to breathe and therefore having the abundant life God promises.

Luke tells us in the second chapter of Acts that on the Day of Pentecost that disciples were all together in one place and suddenly there came from heaven a sound like the rush of a violent wind and it filled the entire house where they were sitting. *Ruach* in Hebrew, which literally means "desert wind," blows through. Doors are blown open, curtains are flapping, shutters rattle back and forth, dust and debris and leaves blow. Wind, *ruach*—and then fire among them. In the confusion they were filled with the wind, the breath of God, and all of a sudden they have power and courage and love more than fear. They began to speak and hear in one another's languages as they spoke of God's great and might works.

The wind blows where it chooses and we do not know where it comes from or where it goes, as Jesus told Nicodemus. In other words, we don't know what will happen so hold on to your hats and get ready to be blown in new directions. Get ready to breathe like you've never breathed before!

The whole book of Acts is this Spirit of God blowing and giving breathe to Samaritans, God-fearers, eunuchs, and Gentiles, crossing boundaries, reconciling, healing, and making whole. Everyone who is hemmed-in, cut-off, cut-out, exiled, ostracized, labeled, marginalized, clamped-down, beaten down, ground down, intimidated, and afraid. To everyone who is being choked to death, God's Spirit of Life blows and gives breath! Read the book of Acts!

We're in a world that is choking to death and God calls us, God empowers us to go give CPR, mouth-to-mouth resuscitation. God calls and God empowers us to be bold, to be brave to go out there where people are being choked to death. God calls us to inhale God's breath and in turn, go out and breathe, exhale into the choking-to-death world.

We're in a world choking to death on racism, choking on guns, choking on hatred and fear, choking on bigotry, choking on hopelessness. People who are impoverished and those in the middle class are choking on debt while the richest are reaping obscene amounts of money.

We have the finest sports arenas and complexes in the world while our public schools suffer from lack of development and our teachers are underpaid, under-appreciated, and over-worked—our children are being choked to death.

We have fewer and fewer people vote in elections because they feel, "What's the use?" while our elected officials find ways to make it harder to vote rather than finding ways to increase voting—our democracy is being choked to death.

The climate is being changed and poor people are the first to have to deal with the consequences but so many of our leaders keep their heads in the sand, while their hands are in the pockets of corporations, all while denying climate change. Our planet is being choked to death.

Into this world the Holy Spirit blows and we are called and empowered to go and breathe, allowing the life-giving breath of God's Spirit to bring life and love, goodness and hope, justice and joy.

Bill Leonard, professor of church history and former dean of the Wake Forest University Divinity School, tells of his special-needs daughter, Stephanie, being baptized at Crescent Hill Baptist Church, in Louisville, Kentucky back when Stephanie was sixteen. Before the worship service was to begin, Stephanie was nervous and Bill and his wife were going to great lengths to help Stephanie be at peace while at the same time they too were anxious. Bill said they were busy checking the water, making sure Stephanie had a change of clothes in the changing room, towels, hair brush, and on and on, when Mildred Burch came up. Mildred was a deacon, a saint of the faith and one of the pillars of the church. She had known Stephanie since Stephanie had been born. Mildred came up and said to Bill, "You all quit doing what you're doing and go out into the congregation and sit where you can see this glorious event. Don't worry about Stephanie; I'll take care of her."

So out Bill and his wife went to sit in the congregation. Stephanie slowly, carefully came down the steps into the water with the help of Mildred and Pastor Steve Shoemaker. Stephanie confessed her faith, "Jesus Christ is Lord" and Steve lowered her under the waters and baptized her in the name of the Father, the Son, and the Holy Spirit. Up she came from the waters, and made her way up the steps to where Mildred Burch embraced her in a big, warm towel and helped her go and dry off and change.

And Bill says, "Mildred Burch embraced Stephanie and breathed upon her. Giving her the Holy Spirit." It was Mildred, and others like Mildred, Sunday school teachers, deacons, ministers, friends, and countless other veterans of the Christian faith who loved Stephanie, embraced her, and breathed upon her the Holy Spirit. Bill adds that Mildred has long since passed to her glory, but the Holy Spirit stills dwells with Stephanie.

There's an image for us to hold in our hearts. This is a picture of the gift given to us and the task that stands before us.

In about ten days Jane and I will make our way to a house in the mountains of North Carolina where we will spend most of the month of June. I need to breathe. I need to adjust to this new CPAP machine and receive increased oxygen and learn to sleep again. But more deeply, I feel as if I'm being choked to death by bigoted religion, mean government, and greedy corporations. What happens is that I am increasingly exhausted and worn-out; I become the mirror of what I oppose. So, I need to breathe. I need to become compliant with the breath the Holy Spirit.

Austin Heights, the Holy Spirit is the gift of God to empower us, renew us, and give us courage. It empowers us to overcome our fears, to be advocates for others, and connects us with God so we will know God more deeply and completely.

Let us breathe.

In the name of the Father, the Son, and the Holy Spirit. One True God, Mother of us all. Amen.

Is America humanly and civilly bankrupt?

The Rev. Martin Luther King, Jr. Annual Banquet

Dayton, Ohio
January 20, 2014

RODNEY WALLACE KENNEDY

When I first learned that I was the back-up to the back-up for this speaking assignment, I said, "Woe is me!" After all, how else would a poor, white, country Southern preacher get this honor? Faced with the task of speaking about Martin Luther King, Jr., I was frightened. I am not a scholar of the African American preaching tradition, even though I have stood hat in hand for more than forty years before that revered pulpit inhabited by Gardner Taylor, and America's preacher, James Forbes. James Cone and Jeremiah Wright have preached for me at First Baptist Dayton. I have often tried to imitate the black preaching tradition, and I am incapable of it, but I'm still trying. My courage received a boost when I remembered the work of racial reconciliation done by my fellow country Baptist preacher, Will Campbell. I dedicate this to Will.

As Vincent Harding has argued, the price for a national holiday to honor a black man seems to be a national amnesia designed to hide from us who that black man really was. So as James Forbes, speaking at a function like this, said: "The opportunity to make this holiday more than just another festive occasion should be a high priority for the religious communities of our nation. At last we have a holiday which makes it an act of patriotism to tell the truth about the basic changes we must make if we are to dream the dream with King." In particular, I think we overlook that Dr. King campaigned against the war in Vietnam, on behalf of the poor, and had a strong commitment to nonviolence.

Racism is not only alive, it is spreading—a gangrene on the conscience of America. Now it includes our treatment of Muslims, immigrants, the poor of all races, gays, and European socialists, especially if they are French. There's a spooky quality about this mysterious time zone in which we are lost: Confederate soldiers, barefoot, starving, marching in ragged lines, rise out of the fog. Long lines of shackled slaves cry out across the bloody landscape. Jim Crow keeps returning dressed in different costumes and making different speeches, but is still the same man. The KKK rises and falls and rises again from the primordial muck of human hatred. After all, it hasn't been quite a century since the KKK held one of their largest rallies at the fairgrounds here in Dayton, and at one time, had 400,000 members in Ohio.[1]

Race is a virus artificially implanted in our civilization at the dawn of modernity and it is so pernicious and so persistent that it shows back up in every generation in a different strain. Like a flu shot that can't account for all the variations of the flu, there's no one antidote that can eliminate racism.

Nothing creates more excitement for a middle-class, middle-aged, white man than someone getting caught in food stamp fraud. When there's a food stamp fraud case, my email box fills with news stories sent to me with love from my conservative Christian friends. No matter that all the alleged food stamp fraud in history doesn't add up to 1 percent of the fraud perpetuated every day by Wall Street investment firms, politicians, media consultants, and investment bankers. A major bank agreed to pay a $12 billion dollar fine for cheating. How much food could that purchase?

And racists are impatient. They think they have done all that needs to be done for African Americans. They ask, with particular bitterness: "What do those people want now?" Listen, for centuries you were denied even the crumbs that fell from the table and Lazarus was your name. And now, the white empire has been forced by law to give the crumbs and the crumbs are not now and will never be enough. We want to all sit at the banquet table with Abraham, Isaac, Jacob, and all the brothers and sisters of the world and enjoy the manna, the abundance of God's economy. We are not here for any damn crumbs; we are here for our portion.

You have to admit that racists have gotten smarter, smoother, more sophisticated, and more dangerous. No longer do racists stand on courthouse steps and scream the "n" word. Principalities are smarter than that.

1. Trollinger, "Hearing the Silence."

In states all over this union elected officials are at work trying to legally take away voting rights. Jim Crow is his name and he hasn't the decency to stay dead! Maybe we could get the cops from the movie *Men in Black* to send Jim Crow to alien hell. The goals of racism never change; only the strategy changes.

And now racists cast their message in economic terms. The proponents of high profits, low taxes on the rich, concentrating wealth and income at the top, and the rest of the trickle-down economics voodoo have a favorite saying: "Don't kill the goose that lays the golden eggs." Starve the poor, but don't kill the goose that lays the golden eggs. Cut benefits, salaries, health care, and housing opportunities, but protect the goose that lays the golden eggs. As historian Robert S. McElvaine, from Mississippi College in Jackson, Mississippi, says, "When profits become too high and taxes on the very rich too low, the geese get obese, eventually stop laying golden eggs, and develop coronary problems."[2]

Historian David W. Blight, in *Race and Reunion*, argues that after the Civil War, white men from the North and the South made a deal with the devil. The North would readmit the South to the union on one condition: everyone agreed to take away the hard-won rights of the newly freed slaves. Both sides, as if they had never been torn apart by war, reunited and went about the systematic denigration of black dignity and the attempted erasure of emancipation from the national narrative of what the war had been about. This gave legal authority for another century of subjugation of an entire people.

Will Campbell said we would make no progress on race until we realized it was a theological problem. Campbell believed the "race problem" had more to do with the universality of human sinfulness and the sovereignty of God than with the secular politics of the day. Will thought the integrationists and segregationists needed repentance. Well, I think Will would have delighted in J. Kameron Carter's book, *Race: A Theological Account*. Carter argues that it was the Christian mistreatment of the Jews that created the metaphorical construct called "race." Christian theology became anti-Semitic and biologized itself so as to racialize itself. This gave birth to the notion of "white supremacy." As a result, Christianity became the cultural property of the West, the religious ground of white supremacy, and global control by colonialism, empire-building, slavery, genocide, and discrimination. And a host of demons followed in the white wake and don't

2. McElvaine, *The Great Depression*, xxxiv.

forget the missionaries blessing the entire evil system. In short, Christianity and colonialism became the Siamese twins of racism. Thus the "race problem," is a theological problem.

So I want to tell you a couple of stories about two Jewish men: Jacob and Esau. Jacob is coming home to face his brother, Esau, and there's a lot that's still unresolved between them. Jacob has stolen everything that wasn't nailed down from Esau. A good Bible story can rise, take up its point, and walk across history from Palestine to Dayton. Using our enlightened imagination let's say it out loud: Jacob is the white man and Esau is the black man.

The narrator wants us to feel the tension of his story. He wants us to believe that Esau is filled with seething resentment and the desire for revenge. "Jacob, Esau is headed this way with 400 men." Feel the fear.

So Jacob sends his wife and children across the creek to face Esau and he brings up the rear. In the 1960s we sent the children to integrate the schools because grown people were not willing to come to grips with the awful evil of racism. Why do we send the children to do our work for us?

The challenge of race is not child's work; this is church, synagogue, and mosque work. This is church work, not public education work. This is church work, not mere secular political work. This is church work, not white and black pastors joining an organization and pretending that we are eradicating racism. And we know why it is so hard for the churches to actually do this work: We fear that it might be the undoing of kingdoms that we have constructed on the sands of times.

Jacob also had a dream. Jacob had a dream of wealth untold and of power beyond compare. His dream had nothing to do with the purposes of God. Not all dreams change people. Even after experiencing God, Jacob is the same old let's-make-a-deal Jacob. "God, If you will give me what I want, take care of my food and clothing, then you will be my God and I will erect a house for you and give a tenth of what you give me."

Esau, it turns out, surprised Jacob. "But Esau ran up and embraced him, held him tight and kissed him. And they both wept." I believe that this has been the response of the African American community to the white community: forgiveness and not revenge. It was by no means certain that nonviolence would win the debate in the African American community. King said, "I'm committed to nonviolence absolutely. I'm just not going to kill anybody, whether it's in Vietnam or here. I plan to stand by nonviolence because I have found it to be a philosophy of life that regulates, not only my dealing in the struggle for racial justice but also my dealings with people and with my own self. I will still be faithful to nonviolence."[3] One race promotes violence; the other race reconciliation and nonviolence. Behold Jacob the white man and Esau the black man. And at its best, black theology has served as a corrective to the inherited privilege and violence of white theology.

There may not be a preacher—white or black—that wants to hear this message in any depth beyond the repeated shouts of "Amen" that have greeted some of my thoughts. I have learned that while "Amen," in the Bible means "So let it be," in our pulpits, the "Amen" has been reduced to "Hmmm, what's for dinner, preacher?" What's for dinner? A table laden with the manna from heaven and all God's children are invited. Is it not time for us to break bread together after centuries of breaking heads and hearts?

I find consolation in the ordinary ways that people of different races minister to one another. My dad died almost two years ago. I feel this loss deeply. On Saturday morning, January 5, 2013, my dad's aid, an African American named Chester, had helped him shower, changed his bedding, fed him breakfast and helped him back into the bed. My dad asked Chester to come over and pray with him. Chester is a part-time bi-vocational Baptist preacher. So Chester held my dad's hand and prayed with him. At the "Amen" Dad crossed his arms over his chest and died. This is what we call a peaceful end. I offer it to you as my continuing participation in Dr. King's dream. A black preacher praying and holding hands with a man named for the president of the Confederacy is irony enough for the deepest skeptic. But there's also this: My dad went to heaven on the sanctified prayer of a black man, on the wings of glorified prayer. And that is enough to keep me in this fight until the scourge of racism, visited upon this planet by an unfaithful version of Christianity (wed unlawfully and in unholy ways to the state and smeared with the violence of colonialism, and a trumped up false metaphor called race), is wiped away.

Amen! And so say we all, Amen!

---

3. From King's speech on the steps of the capital at Montgomery, Alabama, March 25, 1965. See http://kingencyclopedia.stanford.edu/encyclopedia/documentsentry/doc_address_at_the_conclusion_of_selma_march/

What Have We Done with the Good News?

Mark 1

Rodney Wallace Kennedy

We don't know much of what happened to the followers of Jesus from 30 A.D. to around the 50's. Luke gives us information about Christianity moving from Jerusalem to Rome. There's nothing about Christianity in Galilee, precious little about the 12 apostles or the 70 witnesses or the 500 brothers and sisters ("most of whom are still alive") who saw Jesus after his resurrection. Borrowing a bit from Foucault I want to suggest that ordinary, nameless people are the actors in history, the gospel-producers. Glance through the gospel of Mark and meet these nameless people who spread the good news of Jesus before we had any written Gospels.[1]

Let the leper healed in Mark 1 speak for all the ordinary people. Mark says, "He went out and began to proclaim [his healing] freely, and to spread the word." So you think that you are ordinary, that you don't count, that you

---

1. Man with unclean spirit
Simon's mother-in-law
A leper
A paralytic and his four friends
A man with a withered hand
Gadarene demoniac
A woman who had been suffering from hemorrhages for twelve years
The daughter of the leader of the synagogue
Five thousand people fed bread and fish
A deaf man with a speech impediment
Four thousand people fed bread and fish
Little children
Bartimaeus son of Timaeus, a blind beggar
Simon the leper
A woman with a costly jar of oil

haven't ever made a difference? Look at these ordinary people. They kept the gospel alive until Mark could write it down. Listen, you count! You are the spreaders of the good news!

Mark's Gospel was written first.[2] From the beginning, we see that the radical nature of the Gospel made it difficult to swallow whole. The church has a complex and dangerous history of modifying the gospel to align with the culture.

Mark tells us that the good news is that the kingdom of God has come![3] The new kingdom displaces the old kingdoms of nation, religion, and race. It challenges the hierarchies, distinctions, and discriminations of the culture. The kingdom of God brings a radical egalitarianism. The equal sharing of spiritual and material gifts, of miracle and table, cannot be centered only in the here and now, but is always both "here" and "there." Thus the announced radical equalitarianism is rooted in divine initiative past and present. Every wall Jesus breaches, we try to rebuild. Every barrier Jesus knocks down, we try to put back. In the book of Acts, the egalitarianism is in full display. The church selects a replacement apostle for Judas and they do it by lot. A lottery for the twelfth apostle. We understand lotteries, don't we? How many of you dream of winning the mega-lottery? Would you have wanted to win the twelfth apostle lottery? By the end of the first century, the lottery has been displaced with bishops, presbyters, deacons, and all kinds of hierarchical divisions. Now cardinals (a bunch of old men) elect the pope (a man) and the world awaits the puff of white smoke. Imagine the 2016 presidential election decided by casting lots. Put eight candidates from each party in a lottery machine, give it a spin, and pull out a name. And we have a president. Crazy talk, but it would save the Koch brothers a billion dollars and save us a year of mean, awful, painful, lying-through-the-teeth television advertising. The point is that the church struggles to maintain the radical egalitarianism of Jesus.

Let me try to demonstrate from a couple of scenes in Mark 1. When Jesus came to Capernaum, to the house of Peter, he healed Peter's

2. Matthew and Mark had a common source that scholars have labeled "Q" and they each had sources that the other one didn't have. Mark is the most radical teller of the good news.

3. The Greek word for kingdom is *basileia*. "*Basileia* was a common topic of far-reaching significance throughout Hellenistic culture." (Crossan, *Jesus*, Kindle ed., loc. 1125–26.) The ground was thick with kings, emperors, tyrants, and generals. Power and privilege coupled with rights and duties were the hot topics. Kings and rulers had sovereignty, majesty, dominion, power, domain.

mother-in-law and then everyone starting bringing the sick to Peter's house. This is not a disturbing miracle because it is in-house. We are good at in-house gospel stuff: Our family, our people, our place, our nation, and our church. Peter is the first to be called to follow Jesus, the first to suggest a different route. Peter was always trying to get Jesus to change course instead of following. "Get behind me Satan!" Peter grasped the notion that he could become Jesus' broker and help him gather the people and the kingdom would come to pass in Peter's house. Perhaps in some ways, the Roman Catholic Church has never let go of the idea of localizing the church in Peter's house. But Jesus refuses to stay put. "Let us go on to the next towns, so that I may preach there also; for that is why I came out."

Peter argues that it makes more sense to stay at Capernaum, and await the crowds. Peter and Jesus, not for the last time, have different visions of mission. Jesus says, "Go." Peter says "Stay." This is always the tension. Keep the kingdom in Jerusalem would be the cry by A.D. 40. Keep the kingdom for Jews only would be the cry by Acts 15. Keep the kingdom for Catholics only would be the cry of the Middle Ages. Keep America for Americans. Let me ask, "Is your gospel, the one that guides your life, 'made in the USA'?" We prefer in-house gospels. The churches of American are being held hostage by alien politics—alien to the gospel of Jesus.

The message of the gospel confronted social oppression, cultural materialism, and imperial domination in the first and second centuries. The gospel does this work in every century and in every culture. And in every century the church undoes this work or at least tries. This is hard work but we have to keep asking: Are we following Jesus or making up a different gospel?

Mark connects the good news with the healing of a leper. Of all things, the radical move is that Jesus touches a leper.[4] The word translated "leprosy" was a generic term for all skin diseases.[5] To touch a leper was a social mistake, a religious sin, a criminal act. Everyone knew that you didn't touch

---

4. Jesus' practice of touching the leper was a fundamental challenge to honor and shame.

5. "It is certain, first of all, that to translate the Hebrew word *sara'at* or the Greek word *lepra* by the modern term 'leprosy' is flat wrong. What we call leprosy is caused by a bacillus discovered in 1868 by Norwegian physician Gerhard Henrik Armauer Hansen. That disease was in fact known in New Testament times but was then called elephas or epephantiasis. Ancient *sara'at* or *lepra*, on the other hand covered several diseases, all of which involved a rather repulsive scaly or flaking skin condition—for example, psoriasis, eczema, or any fungus infection of the skin." (Crossan, *Jesus,* Kindle ed., loc. 1542–43.)

lepers. Once you touch a man condemned by social structures, you have a social gospel. Are you aware that it was Karl Marx that taught that Christianity conditions people to accept injustice by dreaming of heaven by and by? Hundreds of millions of people have been taught, by Marx and Communism, that Christianity is hostile to concern for social justice for the poor. Given the fact that Jesus' ministry focused on social and economic justice and that he was crucified by the political establishment with the aid of a corrupt religious establishment, a greater lie is hard to imagine. And you have the nerve to call me a socialist. Like touching a long row of standing straight-up dominoes, the touch of Jesus caused all kingdoms, kings, emperors, and empires to fall. The powers and the principalities heard the dominoes falling and they began the conspiracy right then and there that would nail Jesus to a cross.

The culture of Capernaum was built on shame, and the religious leaders had the power to dispense shame. The leper was not a social threat because of medical contagion, threatening infection, or epidemic, but because of symbolic contamination, threatening the security of society at large.[6] Religious people can be shame-spreading experts. They can spread it all around and stack it to the ceiling. Shame sticks to your insides like Velcro; it's shelf life is decades long.

When I was fifteen, a woman ran a red light and hit my car on the driver's side. Her husband owned a local furniture store and he was the first person on the scene because his store was a block away from the accident. He took charge, told the police I was speeding and that was a lie. But what hurt were the words: "He's just a poor white trash kid from the country. Never will amount to anything. It was his fault." My daddy got there and he took care of business in his quiet, humble way. Then he turned to me and saw the tears in my eyes and he grabbed me and hugged me. I didn't even need to tell him what happened; he knew. He hugged me fiercely and whispered, "Son, you are smarter than all of them put together. I love you."

6. In Leviticus 13:45–46: "The person who has the leprous disease shall wear torn clothes and let the hair of his head be disheveled; and he shall cover his upper lip and cry out, 'Unclean, unclean.' He shall live alone; his dwelling shall be outside the camp." You don't have to be a leper to be treated like one. "Torn clothes." Ask any poor middle school student whose parents can't afford name brand-name clothes and shoes and you will hear shame in his voice. According to anthropologist Pierre Bourdieu, "He who has lost his honor no longer exists. He ceases to exist for other people, and at the same time he ceases to exist for himself." (See Bourdieu, "The Sentiment of Honour in Kabyle Society," 211–12.) Those who shame us want us to believe that we can only be what we see through their eyes.

I still have residual resentment from being considered poor and ignorant, but my daddy's words trump those feelings every time. All the way from heaven, I can hear my daddy telling me he was proud of me. And here's a dirty little secret. One of the reasons I loved baseball so much is that it is the great equalizer. Being rich or living in town didn't do those boys one bit of good when I blew two fastballs past them on the outside corner and then when they were leaning over the plate for the next pitch, there came Suzy Q: a vicious dirt-seeking knuckle curve under the hands and the umpire's call of "Strike three!" My first cousin, Junior, dug down in the dirt and nestled that pitch into his catcher's mitt and came up throwing the ball to the third baseman and saying "Atta boy." There's no equalizer like a sharp breaking curve in the dirt.

Why would Jesus risk the resentment of the entire culture? Mark tells us why: *Moved with pity.* He takes the shame of the leper. The good news is not just words but also actions. We too are to be a people of mercy. Spread as much mercy as possible.[7] Put a sign outside our church: "Get your mercy here, America!"

Luke tells a story of Jesus healing ten lepers. Luke portrays Jesus as an observant Jew. Luke puts Jesus back in the cultural box and there he keeps him very well. The lepers keep their distance. Jesus sees them but never comes close enough to touch. Jesus sends the lepers immediately to the Temple. They are healed on the way—no touching. In Mark Jesus touches a leper and destroys cultural boundaries; in Luke Jesus keeps his place in polite society.[8] Jesus died for something more than how we do things around here, something more than the status quo, our cultural rules, customs, habits, and arrangements of power.[9] Crossan says, "To remove that which is radically subversive, socially revolutionary, and politically dangerous from Jesus' actions is to leave his life meaningless and his death inexplicable."

---

7. St. Thomas Aquinas: "In itself mercy is the greatest of the virtues, since all the others revolve around it and, more than this, it makes up for their deficiencies." Showing mercy makes up for all our other deficiencies.

8. There's a warning in the Epistle to the Hebrews about people crucifying Jesus all over again. When we go against the clear teaching of Jesus, when we re-imprison the prisoners Jesus set free, when we exclude the people Jesus included, when we get on our high horse and lord it over people Jesus had lifted up, we crucify again the Son of God.

9. "To remove that which is radically subversive, socially revolutionary, and politically dangerous from Jesus' actions is to leave his life meaningless and his death inexplicable" (Crossan, *Jesus*, Kindle ed., loc. 1799–1800).

Which story do you prefer? Mark's destruction of cultural and religious rules or Luke's culture and religion aligned?[10]

The gospel is the way of Jesus—not my way or your way. The gospel is a way of life—a path to be walked, a set of practices to be embodied in our daily actions. To follow the way of Jesus is an enacted metaphor. It is something we do each new day.

The invitation to follow Jesus is an invitation to take the Jesus way. Perhaps the first four disciples thought they would be home by dinner. It turned out to be far more and maybe that explains why the disciples always seemed to not get it. That is, of course, far different from Jesus' current bunch: We think we know the mind of Jesus about every subject. Did you see the op ed piece in the *New York Times*: "What Would Jesus Do About the Measles?"[11]

There's confusion here because Jesus seems to be going in all directions at the same time. When I went to Minneapolis for the first time, I was confused by the Interstate signs. I-94 WSW completely befuddled me. Not only was I unable to talk "Minnestoan," "yah," but y'all I couldn't read the road signs. How do we know if we are actually following Jesus?

The good news begins with repentance. To repent means to change the mind. Repentance can only happen among people willing to examine their innermost thoughts, motivations, prejudices, and attitudes toward God and others. The "body of Christ" has a split personality. Some of Jesus' followers think we should share the wealth; other of Jesus' followers think that is nasty socialism. Some of Jesus' followers think we should welcome

10. We have invented family values in a gospel that teaches us that the family should be a secondary concern with our following Jesus first. We have invented a form of nationalism that demonizes other religions and other peoples. We have invented a righteousness that makes us superior to all the other nations of the world. We have invested patriotism with spiritual significance and pass it off as a Christian virtue as if that kind of delusion can justify the people we kill. Are we following the gospel or modifying its difficulty to suit our American tastes? Well, our modifying work has been so pervasive I think someone could write a book called *Christian False Gospels of America*. Make a list of what Jesus condemned and see if we have turned those practices into false gospels: nationalism, wealth, and violence.

11. Perhaps you read Paul A. Offit's opinion piece, "What Would Jesus Do About the Measles?" (*New York Times*, February 10, 2015). In 1990, there was a measles outbreak in Philadelphia. The measles outbreak came primarily from members of two churches: Faith Tabernacle Congregation and First Century Gospel Church. "Jesus was my doctor." Of the 1,424 cases of measles, 486 belonged to one of these two churches, as did six of the nine dead children. Offit is a pediatrician specializing in infectious diseases at the Children's Hospital of Philadelphia. He is the author of *Bad Faith: When Religious Belief Undermines Modern Medicine*.

Mexican immigrants, others not so much. Some of Jesus' followers think we are destroying the environment; others that we are inhibiting the economy. Some of Jesus' followers think that the rich getting very, very, very richer while the poor get even poorer is sinful; others that the poor should get jobs and work. Some of Jesus' followers thinks Fox carries news; others not. Some of Jesus' followers think America is God's favorite; others bemoan the idolatry of nationalism. Jesus is not on everyone's side and he may not be on our side. "We are facing division we do not know how to heal." Many may not want to have our alienation from one another healed. "Good people on every side, and there are many sides of every division." I am not sure what to do. I will leave that to you and your willingness to let the gospel read you.

There are plenty of Americans who see no need to confess our national sins. Jonah Goldberg made a recent theological assumption that deserves a moment long enough to consign it to *Sheol*. He claims Americans have the right to sit on our high horse and judge whomever we please. Jesus says, "If I be lifted up I will draw all people unto me." High horse or high cross?[12]

Maybe it is not that we have modified the gospel, maybe it is that our resistance to it has turned us into dragons, and after all these years we have layers and layers of thick gospel-resistant skin. We have to stop being afraid of the radical good news and let Jesus do his work of changing us into his followers. Will you be the radical dispenser of forgiveness, mercy, open sharing, and radical egalitarianism? If so, the gospel is for you.[13]

12. Jonah Goldberg wrote a recent opinion piece entitled "The President's Comparison of Christianity to Radical Islam Defies Logic." Avoiding the political nastiness of the article, I want to shine a theological light on his closing sentence: "I see no problem judging the behaviour of the Islamic State and its apologists from the vantage point of the West's high horse; we've earned the right to sit in that saddle." Goldberg doesn't know that we are not supposed to be sitting on a high horse with a view. The only view that makes us true followers of Jesus is when we are lifted up on a cross. "And I if I be lifted up from the earth will draw all people unto me." As followers of Jesus we have been called to be a blessing to all the nations of the world and yet who did we bomb this morning? We are to be servants to the world. We are to be the Eucharist, the body of Christ, to all the nations of the world. High horse or cross? Which is the gospel?

13. Rowan Williams: "What Jesus was remembered as having stressed was that the kingly rule of God was about to arrive and break in to the human world." "Trust this, live in Jesus' company, and you become a citizen of a new world, a world in which God's rule has arrived." (Williams, *Tokens of Trust*, 58.) You will be free of all the other powers claiming to be ruling. Your life will be a foretaste of God's rule; and it will be directed to inviting as many as possible to come under the same rule, and to resisting the powers and principalities that work against God and seek to keep people in slavery. Jesus was himself the gospel; we are the gospel when we follow Jesus. We are the embodied gospel in the world.

The Gospel Is Relevant

Mark 5:24–34

Will Campbell often lamented that we don't actually trust the gospel. He penned a letter to Grover Bagby of the National Council of Church's General Board of Social Concerns articulating his concerns about the way the NCC was implementing their plan for racial reconciliation. Campbell wrote,

> We just can't quite trust the power of the Gospel message. There just must be something we can add, some gimmick, some technique, some strategy. Just this once I wanted to rely only upon this [the gospel] and if it wasn't enough then let it not be enough. I am more and more convinced that it is enough if our witness to it is faithful. I am likewise more and more convinced that it is all we have to offer as the church.[1]

I offer you this simple claim as affirmation of those 1964 words of Will Campbell:

The gospel is relevant, Brother Will! The gospel is relevant still!

A woman with long-term health issues![2] The gospel is relevant! She spent all that she had on doctors! The gospel is relevant! Jesus healed the woman of her long-term illness. The gospel is relevant! Quite the claim, so let's take a look.

The woman with a twelve-year issue of blood might as well not exist in her time and especially not in ours. In a culture that worships the body, she doesn't count. Terry Eagleton says the body "is the greatest fetish of

1. Campbell, "Letter to Grover Bagby," quoted in Campbell and Goode, *Crashing the Idols*, 27.

2. John Chrysostom (fourth century) notes that the woman was the first woman to approach Jesus publicly and that Jesus uses her faith to correct the lack of faith on the part of the synagogue ruler.

all." Sarah Coakley argues that we are putting our trust in the body and our souls are shriveling.[3] The body, worshiped as god, turns out to have a short shelf life and to be constantly in need of repair, routine maintenance that costs more per hour than a tune-up for a Mercedes, replacement parts, and plastic surgery. And yet we all know what happens to bodies. So this woman's body is ravaged by disease. Her ability to be attractive has been destroyed by years of living in the street, homeless and penniless. She is enslaved by the expected performances of the culture that is the drama of life in the first century. This story matters because this one woman is about to smash to bits centuries of abuse of people as a category of the unclean.[4]

3. This is a gospel story about the human body. The gospel is about flesh and blood. There are gnostic gospels, but the gospel is not gnostic. Our latent gnosticism will likely run screaming from the scene of this woman with a twelve-year issue of bleeding. When I say we are gnostics I am referring to how church people often try to spiritualize every-thing and act as if the body is something foreign and evil. We tend to think that if it is fleshly it must be sinful and that is gnosticism and not what Jesus teaches.

We treat the body as if it were a commodity—another possession we can use as we see fit. There is nothing quite as lonely as believing that the body is all that matters in life. Sarah Coakley, in *Powers and Submissions: Spirituality, Philosophy and Gender*, says: "Why do bodies matter so much? No one can have failed to notice the obsession with the 'body' that has gripped [our] modern popular imagination" (154).Coakely argues that this obsessive interest in the "body" hides a profound longing and that only a theologi-cal vision can satisfy it. No wonder secularism is turning out to be so disappointing to people. Our postmodern secular society with it vehement condemnation of religious faith and meaning has left us with nothing but a body. Think about it—people are putting their trust in bodies and medical science as the meaning of life. And we all know what happens to bodies. From early adolescence, we are victims of the propaganda that our bodies are the meaning of who we are and what we can accomplish. Our only hope seems to reside in keeping the body alive, youthful, consuming, sexually active, and jogging on (literally), for as long as possible. What a cultural contradiction we are: the body is sexually affirmed but puritanically punished in matters of exercise or diet; continuously stuffed with consumerist goods, but guiltily denied foods in the aid of the "salvation" of a longer life. Somewhere the last smile on a Cartesian Cheshire cat still lurks as we engage in this endless dualism.

4. The categories of unclean are clear in Leviticus 18. This story deals with ethical and churchly matters that are part and parcel of current controversies among Christians. For the church has been for several decades deeply divided over levitical issues: the ordina-tion of women and gay marriage. These are levitical issues because they point to the one great question that is central to the vast amount of levitical material found in Torah, namely, what constitutes a holy people? What is the nature and discipline of a commu-nity capable of hosting the presence of God in its midst. For that is what holiness is. It is hospitality toward God, living in such a way that God may feel at home in our midst. The woman's condition clearly marks her as unclean.

The paradigm of what counted as "unclean" is going down. What has felt like predestination is about to be unmasked by an act of free will.

Evicted from her home, fired from her job, refused service at restaurants, uncared for by anyone, she is in solitary confinement. One rule: No touching. The community was afraid. We often act out our fears based on misinformation and then multiply the tragedy by saying that we are just doing what God told us to do.

No one can blame parents for protecting their children. Something drastic occurs when a woman becomes a mother. My grandmother, speaking as a universal mother, often said, "You can mess with me, but don't mess with my children." I get that and I even like it, but we can be overprotective when we continue to insist that some group is going to destroy family life in America.[5]

Scripture was not written in stone! As far as I can tell, the only Scripture ever written on stone was the Ten Commandments and they didn't make it down the mountain in one piece. Scripture is written on the heart and thus it has living, compassionate meanings that you can't wring from a stone. Stone-cold hearts, accusatory fingers wrapped around stone-formed Scriptures. Such monstrous Christianity may turn you, like Medusa, to stone. Only idols/false gods are made of stone. Our God is not a god of stone and the Word of our God is not a word of stone. The boundary keepers who try to keep everyone in their designated place think they are following scared Scripture but may only be worshiping sacred cows. It is not

5. I struggle to understand Christian inability to accept gays. There is so much condemnation and so much preaching that gays are destructive of culture and family. Either these adamant opponents of gays should at least be more honest about the contributions of gays to culture over the centuries. A least some voices ought to be raised as an alternative vision. Why are the voices of the church so filled with condemnation of gays? Why are we bombarded with all the perceived evils that will befall our acceptance of gays? "Aside from their extraordinary contributions to human progress and happiness, what did the following have in common: Erasmus, Leonardo da Vinci, Michelangelo, Christopher Marlowe, King James I, Sir Francis Bacon, Thomas Gray, Frederick the Great, Margaret Fuller, Tchaikovsky, Nijinsky, Proust, A. E. Housman, W. H. Auden, Willa Cather, and Bill Tilden? They were all homosexuals" (Coffin, *The Collected Sermons of William Sloane Coffin,* 450). Preachers are claiming the judgment of God will fall on us for accepting gays. I must dissent. I must offer you a different voice on this issue. I believe the grace of God trumps this alleged judgment. The Supreme Court is going to rule by the end of June on the issue of gay marriage. If the justices strike down the state laws against gay marriage, I want you to know that I will gladly officiate at the marriage of gay couples who meet the requirements that all other couples meet for matrimonial ceremonies in this church. We will be one of sixteen Southern Baptist churches that have so far agreed to do this.

an uncommon problem for God's children. While waiting for the word of God to come down Mt. Sinai they built a golden calf and worshiped it.

Of all things, on his way to help an important male authority figure with his sick twelve year old daughter, Jesus stops to help a nameless woman. Jairus, the male leader is a synagogue official;[6] the woman is excluded from the religious community. As leader of the synagogue he probably wrote the decree that expelled her from the synagogue. It would have happened

6. Jairus represents all boundary keepers in all place and all ages. Boundary keepers think they are the good people in this story. They are protecting the tradition and claiming that the tradition is in line with Scripture. Their hearts are cold but their consciences are clear. They are just doing what the Bible tells them to do. This is what people have always believed. What if we are only keeping alive shame and disgrace? Jesus has also read Leviticus and he has interpreted the ritual rules of uncleanness differently.

There's a prequel to this story. Mark is telling a story about an important religious official and then he stops to tell a story about a woman who is ill. Then he picks up the story about the religious leader again. This "sandwich" arrangement is characteristic of Mark's writing. We have to meet the people who put the woman in this awful predicament. Call them boundary keepers. These are the people who cast her out of the synagogue and gave her a death sentence. One of their representatives is in the story. His name is Jairus: the ruler of the synagogue. It is sweet irony that this religious leader, this important man has to stop and wait and watch as Jesus gives his full and undivided attention and care to a nameless, voiceless, powerless, worthless woman. Jairus was probably leader of the synagogue who read out loud the proclamation that sent this woman into exile.

The woman had a medical condition not a sinful condition. The sin wasn't in the woman; it was in her culture and the boundary keepers of her culture. Boundary keepers are always going on about how much they love sinners. I wonder how many times this poor woman heard it. "I love you, but you can't stay here." "I love you but I can't help you." It is abuse for a preacher to rant about people being an abomination, and then leave the pulpit and say, "But I love you so much. I love you more than life itself." If you can't trust the words of love, you don't have to believe the words of condemnation.

What the boundary keepers lacked was the understanding that there's a difference between disease and illness (see Crossan, *Jesus*). Disease sees the problem, unrealistically, on the minimal level; illness, realistically, on the wider level. Think, for example, of the difference between curing the disease or healing the illness known as AIDS. The cure for the disease is absolutely desirable, but in its absence, we can still heal the illness by refusing to ostracize those who have it, by empathizing with their anguish, and by enveloping their sufferings with both respect and love. The woman had a disease; her culture a sickness unto death. The illness was in the social stigma attached to the woman of uncleanness, isolation, and rejection. We can be so devastated by the rules of the boundary keepers that we confuse them with the word of God instead of the fallible rhetorical construction they are.

Jesus heals the disease and the illness. We are not able to heal diseases or work miracles like Jesus. But we can heal the illness of our culture. The healing that we can offer is an intervention in the social world. How does this provide healing? We can refuse to accept the disease's ritual uncleanness and social ostracization. Jesus said, "You claim this woman is unclean; I say unto you she is whole and pure."

twelve years ago.[7] So at the time that he celebrated the gift of life in a beautiful new daughter, he gives a virtual death sentence to a woman condemned as unclean. Jairus has a family and a large household; she is alone in the world. He is rich; she is impoverished by payment of doctors' fees. He was somebody: ruler of the synagogue. She was nobody.

Listen for a moment to the woman. Her lips are moving as she engages in self-conversation. Mark is not an omnipotent narrator in this story. He can't read the minds and motivations of the characters in his story. This may be an eyewitness account, a testimony the woman later offered to Mark. "She was saying to herself" means muttering in a half-crazed, numb condition. We all talk to ourselves, especially when desperate or in danger. Self-talk can be a necessary survival technique. But we need more than self-talk. Like this woman, we need to reach out to the healing power of Jesus for support.

Look at her! She is so horrendous our eyes dart away as if one of those ads depicting a skeletal, starving child in Ethiopia is on the screen. Mark piles up seven consecutive participles and they roll off the tongue in a slow beat like a funeral dirge: And a woman *being* in a flow of blood for twelve years, and *having endured* many treatments from many doctors, and *having spent* all her money on them and not *having benefited* at all but rather *having gotten worse, having heard* about Jesus and *having come* behind him in the crowd, touched his garment. Then the word "touched" explodes into the room![8] Action now!

"She had heard about Jesus, and came up behind him in the crowd and touched his cloak, for she said, "If I but touch his clothes, I will be made well." This woman has some odd beliefs. Don't we all? Yet, in spite of her inadequate beliefs, she is healed. Isn't it amazing how little faith is required for a miracle? I wonder why we are so insistent that people have more faith and more doctrinal purity. Why can't we quit fussing and get on with the faithfulness? Here's a faith that has heard about Jesus, and just to add a bit of flavor she has some magical notions and some superstition. She believes

7. Joel Marcus suggests the "twelve" is the key word that caused Mark to tie the stories of Jairus and the woman with the issue of blood together. This is an example of the "sandwich" arrangement frequently employed by Mark as a rhetorical strategy. Can there be a greater sense of justice than the synagogue leader having to watch Jesus heal a woman that he, the boundary keeper, had declared unclean? It is like a condemned man released from prison once DNA evidence proved that he was innocent.

8. This is an act of resistance against religious authority. And it has the blessing of Jesus.

she must come into physical contact in order to be cured by him. Faith is always a mixed bag even if you are pretty certain about well, everything.

Read the medical chart: "Immediately her hemorrhage stopped; and she felt in her body that she was healed of her disease." Now look at her again! Can you guess why her chin is lifted? "Why does she breathe as if to show exactly how it's done? Why should both her shoulders, usually quite bent, brace so square right now?"[9] She is the vanguard of a new world for women and wherever women are still treated as less than equal she is there as the standard bearer. She is guarding the world for women! And it all started with a touch—a rebellious touch in defiance of the boundary keepers.

But immediately Jesus, knowing in himself that power had gone out of him, turned in the crowd and said, "Who touched my clothes?" Jesus sensed that power had gone out from him. There is a flow of power that is so free, so open to the world of agony and suffering, that when Jesus is touched, his power responds faster than a Japanese super train. Get close to Jesus and touch him and the power is unleashed. There can't be a better first step for a troubled soul to take. You will touch the source of all the creative energy in the universe, the energy God unleashed billions of years ago for our well-being and salvation. All this energy continues unabated—the goodness of God still looking for places to plug in and make a difference. This is surely the good news the world is dying to hear. Need is the only criteria, not value or worth or status.

"Who touched me?" The question is rhetorical and doesn't suggest a lack of knowledge. In the Greek text it reads that Jesus "continued to look around to see her who had done this." Jesus sensed she was unclean, desperate. He knew and yet the power, without prejudice, without checking to see if this person was on the approved list, went out. Whoosh! The power is released to meet the need. The old authority figures, the people who make it their business to scare us about violating their stone rules, make it their business to say this unclean woman's touch will destroy the power of Jesus' healing. Well, it's time to straighten up and fly right! The power of Jesus is greater than the lies of the boundary keepers. What matters in the gospel is more the healing power of Jesus than our obsession with matters of uncleanness. The power of uncleanness turns out to be a human, rhetorical construction, a human judgment that has no power except that granted

9. Gurganus, *White People*, 138.

by a willing majority to treat people as unclean. The power of Jesus always overcomes the power of a people depending on words written in stone.

"But Jesus continued looking around to see the woman who had done this." Jesus concentrates on the woman whose need has caused her to reach out to him. The focus of Jesus is on the woman not on the words written in stone that had condemned her. The self-awareness of the woman and of Jesus is just remarkable. "She knew in her body." "Jesus, knowing in himself that power had gone out of him." What a deep connection—a visceral, human, fleshly connection between a woman's need and a Savior's power.

Now, hear the good news: "Daughter, your faith has made you well; go in peace, and be healed of your disease."

What does this mean for us? Our imperfect, mixed up notions of faith can bring forth the healing power of Jesus. When need reaches out to us, we can direct the flow of Jesus' power, grace, and mercy in its direction. Instead of cold stone we can be a people of the heart to meet all this human need. The gospel is relevant!

Bibliography

Adams, Noah. *Piano Lessons: Music, Love, and True Adventures.* New York: Dell, 1997.

Aquinas, Thomas. *Summa Theologiae.* http://www.logicmuseum.com/authors/aquinas/summa/Summa/IIb-27-33.htm#Q30a4arg1>.

Berry, Wendell. "About Civil Disobedience." In *It All Turns on Affection: The Jefferson Lecture and Other Essays,* 103–9. Berkeley, CA: Counterpoint, 2012.

Blight, David W. *Race and Reunion: The Civil War in American Memory.* Cambridge: Belknap Press of Harvard University Press, 2001.

Bourdieu, Pierre. "The Sentiment of Honour in Kabyle Society." In *Honor and Shame: The Values of Mediterranean Society,* edited by John G. Peristiany, 191–241. Chicago: University of Chicago Press, 1966.

Branch, Taylor. *Parting the Waters: America in the King Years 1954–1963.* New York: Simon & Schuster, 1988.

Buttrick, David. *Homiletic: Moves and Structures.* Philadelphia: Fortress, 1987.

Campbell, Will D. *And Also with You: Duncan Gray and the American Dilemma.* Franklin, TN: Providence House, 1997.

———. *Forty Acres and a Goat: A Memoir.* Atlanta: Peachtree, 1986. Reprint, Eugene, OR: Wipf & Stock, 1998.

———. *The Glad River.* Macon, GA: Smith & Helwys, 2005.

———. *Soul Among Lions: Musings of a Bootleg Preacher.* Louisville: Westminster John Knox, 1999.

———. *Up to Our Steeples in Politics.* Eugene, OR: Wipf & Stock, 2005.

Campbell, Will, and Richard C. Goode. *Crashing the Idols: The Vocation of Will D. Campbell (and any other Christian for that matter).* Eugene, OR: Cascade, 2010.

Carter, J. Kameron. *Race: A Theological Account.* Oxford: Oxford University Press, 2008.

Coakley, Sarah. *Powers and Submissions: Spirituality, Philosophy and Gender.* Oxford: Blackwell, 2002.

Connelly, Thomas L. *Will Campbell and the Soul of the South.* New York: Continuum, 1982.

Conroy, Pat. *My Reading Life.* New York: Doubleday, 2010.

Cox, James W. *The Twentieth Century Pulpit: Outstanding Sermons by Thirty-Seven Pulpit Masters.* Nashville: Abingdon, 1978.

Crossan, John Dominic. *Jesus: A Revolutionary Biography.* New York: Harper Collins e-books, 2009.

Danielou, Jean. *From Shadows to Reality.* Translated by Wulstan Hibberd. Scotts Valley, CA: CreateSpace Independent Publishing Platform, 2011.

Dickinson, Emily. *The Complete Poems of Emily Dickinson.* New York: Little, Brown, 1960.

Donahue, John R., and Daniel Harrington. *The Gospel of Mark*. Sacra Pagina. Collegville, MN: Liturgical, 2005.

Goldberg, Jonah. "The President's Comparison of Christianity to Radical Islam Defies Logic. *National Review*. http://www.nationalreview.com/article/398030/horse-pucky-obama-jonah-goldberg.

Gurganus, Alan. *White People*. New York: Vintage, 1990.

Hauerwas, Stanley. *Working with Words: On Learning to Speak Christian*. Eugene, OR: Cascade, 2011.

hooks, bell. *Belonging: A Culture of Place*. New York: Routledge, 2009.

Ketchin, Susan. *The Christ-Haunted Landscape: Faith and Doubt in Southern Fiction*. Kindle ed. Jackson, MS: University Press of Mississippi Press, 1994.

Kruse, Kevin M. *One Nation Under God: How Corporate America Invented Christian America*. New York: Basic Books, 2015.

Lischer, Richard. *The End of Words: The Language of Reconciliation in a Culture of Violence*. Grand Rapids: Eerdmans, 2005.

Marcus, Joel. *Mark. Mark 1–8*. Anchor Yale Bible. New Haven: Yale University Press, 2009.

McElvaine, Robert S. *The Great Depression: America, 1929–1941*. 3rd ed. New York: Three Rivers, 2009.

Miller, Kenneth R. *Only A Theory: Evolution and the Battle for America's Soul*. New York: Penguin, 2008.

O'Connor, Flannery. *The Habit of Being: Letters of Flannery O'Connor*. Edited by Sally Fitzgerald. New York: Farrar, Straus and Giroux, 1988.

Osherow, Jacqueline. *Dead Men's Praise*. New York: Grove, 1999.

Ramsey, G. Lee. *Preachers As Misfits, Prophets, and Thieves: The Minister in Southern Fiction*. Louisville: Westminster John Knox, 2008.

Taylor, Barbara Brown. *When God Is Silent*. Lanham, MD: Rowman and Littlefield, 1998.

Tompkins, Jerry R. *D-Days at Dayton: Reflections on the Scopes Trial*. Baton Rouge, LA: Louisiana State University Press, 1965.

Trollinger, William. "Hearing the Silence: The University of Dayton, the Ku Klux Klan, and Catholic Universities and Colleges in the 1920s." *American Catholic Studies* 124 (Spring 2013) 1–21.

————. "The History of First Baptist Church." http://www.fbcdayton.org.

Turner, Michael A., and William F. Malambri III, eds. *A Peculiar Prophet: William H. Willimon and the Art of Preaching*. Nashville: Abingdon, 2004.

Williams, Rowan. *Tokens of Trust: An Introduction to Christian Belief*. Louisville: Westminster John Knox, 2007.